SPLINTERS OF LIGHT

SPLINTERS OF LIGHT

FRANK TOPPING

ISBN 978-1-905958-21-4

First published by Inspire
4 John Wesley Road
Werrington
Peterborough PE4 6ZP

Typeset by Regent Typesetting, London
Printed and bound in Great Britain by
www.printondemand-worldwide.com
Peterborough

Contents

Introduction

As a young man, straight out of the RAF, I joined the Leatherhead Repertory Theatre company. For about two years I was involved in a different production every week. The range of plays was huge, from contemporary theatre to Restoration comedy, from Whitehall farce to Greek tragedy.

In the Greek play *Hippolytus*, by Euripides, a young and willowy Vanessa Redgrave played the goddess Aphrodite. I played 'Fourth Huntsman', and was also in charge of the lighting, which was a considerable responsibility. The director wanted the play to start in complete darkness. Blackouts are notoriously difficult to achieve in a theatre because the smallest chink of light will defeat any darkness. The task of tracing and covering every last chink of light was extremely difficult – but we did our best.

Each night the house lights faded, and soft, slightly sinister music began as the curtain lifted on a completely blacked-out stage. The audience held its breath in the eerie atmosphere. Suddenly a high-pitched violin note pierced every ear, and at exactly the same moment a 'splinter' of light struck the face of a statue suspended high up above the stage. The audience gasped, every eye riveted on that disembodied alabaster face. Gradually the light on the statue began to fade, as a second light grew to reveal the figure of Vanessa Redgrave, dressed in exactly the same costume and standing in exactly the same pose as the statue of Aphrodite above.

It was a breathtaking experience of theatre. In one instant we were transported from the mundane and commonplace into a different time and place: the presence of Aphrodite and Zeus and the ethereal world of Greek mythology, and all this before even a word had been spoken. The moment I have described took place more than 50 years ago, but that startling image revealed by a splinter of light is as vivid in my mind as it was on the first night I saw it. I doubt if anyone who was there has forgotten it either.

I could not have known then that, in a few years' time, as a student I would be drawn into the study of Theology and Church History, into New Testament Greek and the world of Jewish and Christian Scripture, into a spiritual journey where I would experience similar, breathtaking 'splinters of light', when my mind awakened to awesome possibilities. Later I would share in the experience of other men and women who knew that at a particular moment they too had been touched by something strange, beautiful and infinite – spiritual experiences which are by their nature impossible to put into words.

We are all creatures of time and space. We live in a world measured by years, months, days, hours and seconds. We cannot live in the past or the future; we are imprisoned in the 'now'. If today is Tuesday, it is 2 p.m. and it is raining, no amount of thinking and wishing will take us back to Monday at 10 a.m. when the sun was shining. 'Now' is the only time – or is it?

Imagine instead the idea of two realities: the 'now' world, and a world not limited or confined by either time or space, the 'eternal'. In the stories and experiences described in the Bible it is as if these two worlds are separated by a very fine and thin veil. Every now and then a tiny rent occurs in the veil, and a 'splinter of light' shines through. Those who share these moments are changed by them for ever. I am convinced that such moments of inspiration and insight still occur today, but it seems to me that they have never occurred with such frequency and intensity as in the days when Jesus walked the streets of Nazareth or wandered in the hills of Galilee.

Reading the New Testament reveals that the retelling of extraordinary events of the gospel by ordinary men and women was very difficult. Words seemed to fail them, and they used phrases such as 'It was as if'; 'He seemed to'; 'It was like'.

Look at the story of the Transfiguration (Matt. 17.1–9; Mark 9.2–9; Luke 9.28–36). Peter, James and John go up a mountain with Jesus. Exactly what happened while they were there we may never know. Jesus charges them not to tell anyone what they have seen until after he has risen from the dead, and although they discuss what he means with each other, they do indeed keep it to themselves. When eventually they do tell their story it is with great difficulty: Jesus' appearance was changed; it seemed to shine like the sun; his garments seemed to glow whiter than can be imagined; and then he had a conversation with two men from the past: Moses and Elijah. Of course, in normal experience this is not possible, but in this story the now and the eternal appear to have merged.

Pentecost (Acts 2.1–4) is another such occasion when people struggled to explain the inexplicable. The disciples were behind locked doors in Jerusalem when suddenly there was the sound of a mighty wind, filling the whole house. People gathered in the city were so amazed by the sound that they ran out into the street. The whole experience is described in so few words, but it was a moment of seismic change for the disciples. Something happened that changed frightened and confused men and women into bold and fearless witnesses who went out and ultimately turned the world upside down. So what happened? If it had been a 'mighty' or, as the original text says, 'a 'violent' wind, it would have been foolhardy and dangerous for people to have ventured into the street, but that is what they did. They had indeed heard something that sounded like a mighty wind, but, in fact, what they had was something entirely different.

Next, tongues of flame seemed to touch the heads of everyone in the upper room. When I was a small boy in a Merseyside Anglo/Irish Catholic community, I served as an altar boy, frequently in candlelit processions. I know exactly what happens when flame touches hair. In the upper room at Pentecost it may have looked like tongues of flame, but it could not have been flames as we know them. In their descriptions of both the wind and the flame, they were trying to put into words a spiritual experience, in which they were struck by splinters of light from that other dimension, the eternal.

The story of Mary Magdalene's Easter morning encounter outside the tomb in the garden (Jn. 20.11–18) is another attempt to describe an experience that defies description. Mary had been with the others who had stood at the foot of the cross. She had watched Jesus die. She would have known every inch of his face, yet here, a matter of hours later, she does not recognize him and mistakes him for the gardener. Mary was in her own time and space, her now, and it is as if Jesus drew back the veil to let in the eternal with a single word: 'Mary'. In that moment she recognized him.

Later the same evening, two of Jesus' followers, probably Cleopas and his wife Mary, were walking to their home at Emmaus (Lk. 24.13–35). Suddenly they were aware that a third person was walking with them, and like Mary Magdalene they did not realize that it was Jesus. People have suggested that Mary Magdalene did not recognize Jesus because she was blinded by her tears, but the two people on the Emmaus road walked with him for miles, and still did not recognize him until, I believe, he chose to reveal himself. This time he does not reveal the eternal with a word but with an action. He breaks bread and at that moment, not merely a splinter but a shaft of light bursts into their consciousness. In the breaking of bread they see the risen Christ with them at their table.

At every service of Holy Communion, when the bread is broken a splinter of light from the eternal illuminates our now. Jesus did not say, 'Whenever you sit around a table and within a particular liturgy recite the story of the Last Supper and say particular prayers, then I will be with you.' His legacy to us is more generous. Whenever we break bread in his name, we are truly in 'Holy Communion' with the risen Christ. Ever since that first Holy Communion, millions of splinters of light have cascaded into the hearts of people throughout the world, to all who break bread in his name.

Thanks be to God.

Frank Topping
May 2008

Agnostics up the river

Some years ago I received a letter from an old friend, who described her attitude to God and religion as agnostic, though that didn't mean she was indifferent. It didn't mean sitting on a fence and 'opting out'. For her, being agnostic was stressful, as she felt unable to move in one direction or another intellectually. 'What do you feel,' she asked, 'about agnosticism as an intellectual stance?' I did my best to be rational, but I always find it difficult to discuss ideas without using allegories and parables. This is fine, providing you don't drop the proverbial paddle whilst up the proverbial creek. Anyway, this was my reply:

Dear T.

The expression 'sitting on the fence' frequently suggests the avoidance of making a decision. It may be true that some people use the agnostic label as an excuse for avoiding any kind of serious thought, a thin disguise for 'mental anaemia', as it were. But for someone who, after a great deal of thought and discussion, is genuinely stuck on the fence, it is undoubtedly a painful and unenviable position. Though I have to say that anyone who continues to ask the question 'Why?' with regard to the meaning of things is, inevitably, to some extent, agnostic. It is not the people who don't know the answers who worry me, but those who think they do. Those who have got the whole 'source and meaning of life' thing buttoned up, whether or not they have used theological or scientific buttons, I'm afraid are suspect to me. I'm instinctively wary of absolute convictions, of any kind. Fundamentalists, scientific, artistic or theological, always beg questions.

Unfortunately, jumping off the fence does not mean that you automatically fall into the supportive arms of faith, and there are times when one longs for the security that the fence seems to offer. For some it can be a nerve-racking step into the dark, in the hope of finding something solid under their feet, some light around the corner. For some it is the beginning of a perilous exploration of a vast uncharted continent. What information there is, is confused by superstitious tales and centuries of ancient myths. It's like searching for the source of some great surging river that has a thousand tributaries, and at the end of various creeks and inlets legions of myopic explorers are shouting, 'It's here! We've found it!' Sometimes people are pitched out of their frail canoes and almost overwhelmed by the swirling waters of doubt and cynicism; indeed, some people drown.

Perhaps it is oversimplifying the argument to say that the difference between the searching agnostic and the searching believer is that the agnostic says, 'I have not seen any light to indicate the direction in which I should travel', whilst the believer says, 'I too am in the dark, but I believe I saw something over there.'

If I have any disenchantment about people who call themselves either agnostics or believers, it is because I know that there are both agnostics' canoes and believers' canoes that have never actually left the bank. I think *you* have cast off from the bank with very serious intent. I suspect that you may be stuck up a particular creek at the moment, but I also believe Blaise Pascal was right when he said, 'To seek God, is to find him.' So keep paddling! You never know what you might find up the next creek.

Love, F.

Lord, in your mercy, give courage
to those who find it difficult to believe or
    to pray:
to those who have lost a faith they once
    possessed
or those who doubt not only your love, but
    your very existence.
May your Holy Spirit enlighten our minds
    and lead us into all truth,
        through Jesus Christ, our Lord.
Amen.

Angels

My mother once saw a musical called *Twenty Million Sweethearts*, starring Dick Powell and Ginger Rogers. She remembered very little about the story except for one song, which she sang to me when I was a baby. She was still singing it when I was a grown man, and in her old age, if I said to her, 'Give us a song, Mum', she would look me in the eye and sing:

> You may not be an angel,
> 'cos angels are so few:
> but until the day that one comes along,
> I'll string along
> with you.

Angels loomed large in my mother's view of the world, as they have always done in songs and Hollywood movies. One of the best Christmas movies, *It's a Wonderful Life*, features James Stewart sorting his life out with the help of an angel called Clarence. More recently I watched John Travolta as the Archangel Michael, and Nicolas Cage as an angel falling in love with Meg Ryan in *City of Angels*; and Robbie Williams sings about his 'Angel' Mum.

Why are angels so fascinating? And what is an angel anyway? One definition says that angels are messengers from God who bring good news, or help, at just the right moment. If that is so, then my wife and I were once helped by an angel, when we were robbed on the Tangentiale, the ring road around the north of Naples. We had been tricked into getting out, and looking at the back of the vehicle while someone else jumped in at the front, grabbed my wife's bag, ran across several lanes of motorway, threw himself into a waiting car and sped away. We were distraught. The bag contained passports, our ferry tickets home and most of our money. Further down the motorway we spotted a couple of Caribineri, local policemen, standing by their car. We approached them and then realized what else had been in the bag: the Italian phrase book.

We spoke no Italian and they spoke no English. A crazy pantomime of wild gesticulations followed and, just as we thought it was all hopeless, another car drew in. The driver got out saying, 'I saw your GB plates; I am Italian but I teach English. Can I help?' Now, he *was* an 'angel', arriving with help at just the right moment. We didn't get our bag back, but we did find a friend when we needed one.

Looking back, I think my life has been blessed by 'angels' turning up when I needed them. I expect you've come across a few angels yourself, or, come to think of it, you might have been an angel for someone else.

Lord, you have blessed my life with
*   'angels'.*
When the time is right may I have the
*   courage*
to 'be an angel', to help, love or serve in
*   your name.*
Amen.

Anselm: faith and understanding

I once made a number of broadcasts on the BBC with a famous policeman, John Stalker. I thought Stalker was a wonderful name for a detective. I had always imagined detectives to be 'stalkers', sharp-witted, shrewd people like Sherlock Holmes, who 'stalked' their prey down dark alleyways and ill-lit streets, picking up clues and intelligently analysing facts and human nature until they arrived at some irrefutable truth.

The first time John and I talked together on the radio, however, we did not discuss crime, instead we talked about patron saints, such as St Cecilia, the patron saint of musicians, and St Christopher, the patron saint of travellers. It occurred to me to ask John if there was a patron saint of detectives. He couldn't think of any dedicated to his particular profession. Then suddenly, I remembered St Anselm.

When I was a schoolboy I attended a school called St Anselm's. St Anselm had been the Archbishop of Canterbury, and our school motto was a quotation from one of his works, *Fides Quaerens Intellectum*, which means faith seeking knowledge, or understanding. 'After all,' I said, 'that is what detectives are doing all the time, isn't it, searching for understanding, for the truth, for knowledge?'

Anselm's strong point was argument. He was a great theologian and philosopher but he was different from all his predecessors in that he preferred to defend the faith by intellectual reasoning instead of scriptural arguments. For instance, he argued that the existence of God could be established from the consideration of truth and goodness as intellectual notions. He was responsible for one of the most famous intellectual ideas about the existence of God, known as the ontological argument. Basically it asserts that if you can conceive of a being that cannot be surpassed by anything greater, then that 'being' is God.

Whether we agree with Anselm's arguments or not, we can all sympathize with his desire to find a rational and reasonable expression of his faith. Although he was an intellectual whose life was governed by logical argument and rational philosophy – even reading his prayers you are aware of his searching and questioning mind – he was nevertheless a very devout man. In this piece of devotional writing he sounds like, well, a detective at prayer?

Everywhere you are wholly present,
and yet I see you not.
In you I move and have my being,
yet cannot come to you.
You are with me and about me,
yet I feel you not.

Lord, teach me to seek you
and reveal yourself when I seek,
for I cannot seek you unless you teach me,
nor find you except you reveal yourself.
Let me seek you in longing,
let me long for you in seeking:
let me find you in love
and love you in finding.
Amen.   Anselm 1033–1109

Behind the mask

I read about a drama festival in which various youth theatre companies performed new plays written especially for the festival. One company, from an all-boys school, was somewhat surprised to find that their play, set in ancient Japan, required an all-female cast. They were shown illustrations of traditional Japanese theatre which revealed that the actors used a very stylized make-up, so ornate that it was the equivalent of playing behind masks. They also discovered that in the ancient Japanese theatre there were no female actors.

Even though they used the mask-like make-up, the story was still about a group of women, and the boys still had to try to understand the thoughts, actions, hopes, dreams and emotions of the characters they were playing. I'm sure, educationally, it did them a lot of good, and there must have been a great number of searching conversations with sisters, mothers and girlfriends.

At one time I worked as a school chaplain and taught at a girl's boarding school. We had a training weekend in which, at one session, we were asked to deal with some of the issues and situations that arose in that kind of closed community, but from the point of view of the pupils, to put ourselves, as it were, in their shoes.

It was a very revealing exercise, and there was much heated debate about what really went on in the minds and hearts of our young charges. I'm sure it helped us to be far more thoughtful and considerate when we were face to face with them in the school.

Putting yourself in someone else's shoes does help you to understand their situation more and to sympathize with their needs and difficulties. And that is what Christians believe happened when Jesus walked the streets of Jerusalem, Bethany and Nazareth. He identified himself with human frailty and need, so that when we stand before God in our prayers, we have a friend at court, an advocate, someone who has first-hand experience of our situation and who speaks on our behalf out of his sympathy for our very human problems. When we pray it helps to remember that Jesus understands sorrow, pain and grief, he knows our situation, and prays with us.

> *Jesus, son of Mary, friend of the sick, the weary, sinner and outcast, through your love and understanding of our humanity, you have reconciled us with the Father. Help us to understand and be reconciled with our sisters and brothers, and to walk in the shoes of all those we have been given to love.*
> *Amen.*

Being alone

I remember a song of Frank Sinatra's, which described the haunting feeling of being lonely in a crowd. At that time, I knew what he meant. I was a young man in London, looking for work. My wife and our first-born child were in the Midlands and London seemed a very lonely place. I remember looking at the people in the street, all striding purposefully; people who seemed to belong; people who had jobs and homes. I felt I was an outsider, a loner who had no place there.

That loneliness was temporary, and sometimes it is good to be alone, but real loneliness is an emptiness that aches and hurts like hunger. The emptiness of bereavement, for example, creates a permanent void, and those who have been deserted are wounded; even when the wound heals a scar remains. Some people are lonely in their marriage, or even in their families. Behind the lighted windows of many city apartments are people locked in prisons of shyness, guilt and in-adequacy; solitary not by choice, in kitchens, bed-sits or luxury hotels.

In some places people are put into solitary confine-ment as a punishment. Some regimes place those who oppose them under house arrest, and people are sometimes forced to live in that form of isolation for years. People who have survived solitary confinement for long periods say that they needed to be proactive in order to keep their minds and themselves alive. To do this people have created inner worlds, have reached down inside themselves and found spiritual strength and resources they perhaps did not know they possessed. They have written poetry, songs or even whole books.

The late Dag Hammarskjöld, President of the United Nations, once said, 'Pray that your loneliness may spur you into finding something to live for': words from a man who had been lonely and had learned that waiting for something or someone to come and heal your loneliness can be a very long wait. You need time to come to terms with bereavement, to learn how to live with loss, but in the end you have to take steps to make a different life; you can never be the same again, but you can make a new life.

I once talked with a young woman who had been suddenly widowed and who did not have any children. She said that not only did she lose her husband, she also lost her friends, because people seem to be embarrassed by her grief. Many went through the formality of sending letters of condolence, but after that they seemed to avoid her.

In time she went to a church and asked if she could help by visiting people who were lonely or housebound. Very quickly she became so involved in other people's needs that she was able to adjust to her own loss. Although she could not cure her grief, she found that she could begin to live with it and, more than that, she made new friends and found new purpose.

'Pray that your loneliness may spur you into finding something to live for.'

God of all hopefulness, whose Son, Jesus Christ, suffered the terrible isolation of the cross, give hope and courage to all who suffer loss and loneliness that, inspired by your ever-present love, they may find opportunity to share that love with others, through Christ our Lord.
Amen.

Being content

In his letter to the Philippians St Paul argues that if we concentrate on other people's interests, rather than our own, we will have fellowship with the Holy Spirit and with Jesus Christ, the highest and happiest achievement we could hope for. Therefore, we should try not to be controlled by selfish ambition and pride, which in the end are always unsatisfying. Paul's words are all the more remarkable when we consider that he wrote this letter as a prisoner chained to a praetorian guard.

By chance, I read an article about Charles Dickens' novel *Great Expectations* that came to the conclusion that the novel was really about the hero, Pip, learning of the sufferings and disasters that strew the path of vaunting ambition, pride and self-interest, and that, ultimately, the secret of contentment lay in valuing the things he had *now*, rather than in coveting the things he thought he wanted in order to be happy *in the future*.

And then – as my mother used to say, 'Lo and behold' – by further chance, I picked up a copy of St Teresa of Avila's book *The Interior Castle*, in which she says that most people's unhappiness stems from the fact that they are either living in the past or living in the future. Those living in the past, she says, spend their time regretting that they cannot recapture it, and those living in the future spend their time longing for better things tomorrow, or fearing the disasters that might, or might not, strike. So, Teresa of Avila advises, 'Live in the present.' In other words, value and enjoy what is good in your life now; which, even when he was a prisoner, St Paul seemed able to do.

> *Lord,*
> *free us from anxiety,*
> *help us to give thanks for the past,*
> *trust in you for the future*
> *and live in the knowledge of your presence,*
> *in this and every hour.*
> *Amen.*

Being me

I wonder if, like me, you are inclined to daydream whenever you see an aeroplane flying high above, making for some distant and mysterious foreign destination. I frequently find myself asking, 'I wonder where that aeroplane is going? and wishing I was on it.

It's a mild form of escapism I suppose, the idea that almost anywhere other than where I am at the moment must be more exciting, more interesting, more rewarding. It is also just as easy to wish that you are someone other than who you are. It's a game that children play, but as some of us never grow up we are always wishing that we were taller, or thinner or better-looking. If only we had been born into a different family we might have been richer, more intelligent, more generous, more holy or simply more 'interesting' than we think we are.

One of the basic essentials of coming to terms with what we can do with our lives, what we can hope for, aim at or, to use an old-fashioned expression, recognize as 'our calling', is to accept 'where' we are – and 'who' we are. Every person is unique, and each of us has a role to play or a contribution to make that no one else can offer.

One of the schools our children attended introduced a system of assessment in which children were not given marks that related to what other children were doing; all the marking was related to the individual. They were not in competition with each other, but with themselves. Children were told their work was as good as, or better, or not as good as, work they had done before. So from the child's point of view, they were told, 'It doesn't matter what other children are doing, all that matters is whether or not *you* are holding your ground or improving.'

Henri Nouwen once said: 'We will never find our vocations by trying to figure out whether we are better or worse than others. We are all good enough – to do what *we* are called to do.'

We are all God's beloved children, called to love God and our neighbour in our own time and place and in our own particular way. So, enjoy where you are and who you are. Like yourself, laugh at yourself, enjoy being yourself, and in the process you are quite likely to find God, your neighbour, and your vocation.

Nevertheless, it's still fun to wonder where that plane is going – and to wish you were on it!

> *O God of light and love,*
> *help us to see you in the time and place we*
> *   have been given,*
> *to value our lives in the light of your love,*
> *   to value and enjoy the people we know,*
> *and to find our purpose in and through*
> *   our Lord and Saviour, Jesus Christ.*
> *Amen.*

Being still

I have to confess that as a child I really did not understand the difference between being quiet and being still. In fact, many adults do not really know the difference either. The breakthrough for me came at about the age of 17, sitting in church on an Ash Wednesday afternoon.

Childhood memories of Ash Wednesday stand out in my mind. I don't think I had much idea of repentance and renewal, I just remember the childish delight of having someone make a sign of the cross on my forehead with ashes and wearing the smudge as a mark of distinction. It was customary to give something up for Lent, but I doubt if I really knew why we were doing it. Grown-ups, of course, did it to remind themselves that in Lent, they were required to practise disciplines that might help them to renew and recommit themselves to their Christian pilgrimage.

As a very small child I attended a convent school, where nearly all the teachers were nuns. Now, nuns know about being silent and being still; ah, sure, didn't Sister Philomena have a little mantra that she recited with monotonous regularity? 'God gave me two eyes to see with, two ears to hear with, but only one mouth to speak with, therefore I should see and hear twice as much as I speak.'

Even in those days I was inclined to be argumentative, not that I would have dared to question Sister Philomena, but in my head I would think, 'Two eyes, two ears, one mouth; therefore, you need to speak twice as much to catch up with your eyes and ears.' Had I had the nerve to voice my argument, no doubt she would have said, 'Silence is golden.' Actually, silence can be very disturbing, and because of that most of us like to have the sounds of life around us, for instance, music from the radio.

Anyway, that Ash Wednesday I discovered that being silent is not the same as being still. I had been to confession and at the end I had waited for the priest to give me the usual penitential prayers, when he surprised me by saying, 'I want you to sit and be still in the church for five minutes. I'm not talking about silence, mind, but stillness. Don't say any prayers, just be still in the presence of God.' It was the first time I had ever been asked to consider the difference between silence and stillness.

Being silent, of course, does not stop the voices in your head, the anxieties or the questions that will not go away. Being still in the presence of God requires us to stop asking questions. Being still requires a kind of 'emptying'. You could try to be still by sitting comfortably, just thinking about your breathing. Relax your hands and feet. Take a few deep breaths and, as you breathe out, imagine all your tension, all your stress, draining out of your body, out through your finger-tips and toes. Perhaps you could say to yourself, 'Here I am, in your presence, and nothing else matters but this moment of peace.'

Every day, whether you are sitting at home, or on a bus, or in a waiting-room, a few moments of real stillness in the presence of God, not asking for anything, not pleading, not saying prayers, just emptying yourself and being still could prove far more therapeutic, physically, mentally and spiritually than hard-earned holidays in some far-flung place.

That first Ash Wednesday experience of stillness opened up a whole new world for me, a new way of 'being'. I have a prayer which is about finding spaces in your day to be still. It is a very appropriate spiritual exercise for Lent, but if we try to make a little space at least once a day, in any season, we might begin to learn to be still in the presence of God – and there is no telling where that may lead us.

> *May every day begin with space*
> *enough to see my Saviour's face,*
> *may every hour possess within it*
> *the space to live a prayerful minute.*
> *And may I find from night's alarms*
> *the space between my Saviour's arms.*
> *Amen.*

Bereavement

I have been asked many times over the years: 'What can I say to someone who has lost a life-partner, a husband or wife?' Well, if I were to write on this subject to an imaginary friend, I would say something like this:

Dear Jill

I have just heard about Jack. I am so sorry. Even though we tried to be prepared, it is still a terrible shock. Death is always a shock, whether it is sudden or long expected. Right now, you are probably wrapped in the numbness of grief, and I will understand if you don't feel up to reading this letter. Anyway, it doesn't matter, at least it's there if you should want to read it later.

Your faith is probably far more tested and refined than mine. However, I still think it is a good thing, even for stout-hearted pilgrims like you, to be reminded of what lies at the heart of the Christian faith. The words of the promises of Jesus are very familiar but they take on a special significance at a time like this. He said, 'In my Father's house there are many mansions, and I go to prepare a place for you, so that where I am you may be also.' And he underlined the promise when he said, 'If it were not so – I would have told you.'

St Paul, in his letter to the Corinthians, borrowed some of the poetry of Isaiah when he wrote, 'The eye has not seen, nor the ear heard, neither has it entered our hearts, what things have been prepared for those who love God.'

Above all, remember that our faith is based on the promises of Jesus who, even as he was dying, said to the thief on the cross, 'Today, you will be with me in paradise.' Such is the generosity of the love of God. It is immediate and unconditional – all we have to do is to accept the love that conquers death. Christ's mission was to reveal to the world that the true nature of God was not concerned with punishment, revenge and retribution, but forgiveness, reconciliation and healing. As Paul said to the Corinthians, 'God was in Christ reconciling the world to himself.'

I believe that Paul was right when he said, 'I am convinced that nothing in all creation can separate us from the love of God', but I am equally convinced that nothing can separate us from those whose love and laughter live on in us, in our minds and memories. And that's another thing, don't be afraid of good memories: enjoy them; if they make you cry, then cry, but thank God for them. There is a verse you might find helpful, which reads:

Only love can mourn,
Love that laughed and cried,
Love well-used and worn,
Love that never died.
Love blesses the bereaved,
Love prepares the way,
Love is not deceived
When death has had his say.
Love in Christ puts death to flight,
Love prepares the place
Where love, with love, will all unite
Before that loving face.

God bless you, Jill, and give you all the courage you need at all the times you need it.

Yours ever,

Frank.

Almighty God, grant that those who mourn may enter into the experience of Christ's victory over death and his resurrected life; that in their grief they may be comforted by the knowledge that every joy they have ever known has been but a foretaste of the heavenly banquet prepared for those who have loved you, through Jesus Christ, our Lord.
Amen.

Big seas and small boats

Some people have relationships with God which they find difficult to put into words. Women and men of action often express themselves more in the things they *do* than in the things they *say* but, every now and then, they reveal that the relationship they find difficult to describe is nonetheless profound. It is a spirituality often experienced when people are far away from the artificialities of rich and sophisticated societies. In ancient days the Desert Fathers sought out desolate places in order to clarify their thinking. Jesus, before starting his mission and calling his disciples, spent 40 days in the wilderness.

The sea, of course, is one of the great wildernesses where people have discovered a spiritual awareness that had previously escaped them in the cities and ports they had left behind. When Sir Alec Rose was sailing around the world on his own, he found himself in the Southern Ocean with a desperate problem that required him to climb to the top of the mast, in order to put a vital piece of equipment right. He later said that he could never have done it on his own, but as he went up the mast he became aware that he was not alone. He believes that God was with him in that situation.

I spoke to Clare Francis on her yacht in the days when she was the skipper of a Round the World Yacht Race boat. She talked to me about her experience in earlier days as a lone sailor. When she sailed alone across the Atlantic Ocean, she said, the great problem was that there was no one to keep a lookout while she was sleeping. In an attempt to deal with this she made a habit of sleeping for very short periods, 20 or 30 minutes perhaps, throughout the day and night so that she could check the yacht, the weather and her position. On one occasion she went below to sleep having swept the horizon and seen nothing. Thirty minutes later she came up and as she stepped into the cockpit and looked at the wake of her boat, to her horror she saw that she had sailed exactly between two massive icebergs. At that moment she offered a prayer of thanksgiving. It was a moment of spirituality that was difficult to put into words.

Another, 'round-the-world-solo' sailor, who spoke of his relationship with God while he was at sea, was the Scottish sailor Chay Blyth. I met him whilst making a television programme and we were discussing how, in a sophisticated world, belief in God was no longer considered very fashionable. Chay was sitting opposite me. He was smiling a kind of secret smile and there was a faraway look in his eye. Suddenly the smile disappeared, and he looked up and said, 'Show me a man who doesn't believe in God, and let him come down with me to the Southern Ocean, and see if he's quite so cocky down there.'

It's not a proof of the existence of God, but I know what he means.

Big seas and small boats

Lord, forgive us
that even when most in need
we fail to perceive your presence or hear
* your voice.*
In your mercy, open our inward ears, eyes
* and heart,*
that, in whatever situation we might find
* ourselves,*
we may hear, see and know you,
in and through our Lord and Saviour,
* Jesus Christ.*
Amen.

Blessed assurance

On 24 May 1738, an Anglican clergyman named John Wesley started his day in the City of London in a somewhat depressed state of mind. A few months earlier, he had returned from Georgia, in America, a long journey in those days; in a small sailing ship it could take months. He had travelled in winter and the dark and troubled seas reflected what was going on in his mind. He was troubled because he did not have what he called 'an assurance of belief' in God. Yes, he prayed, preached and celebrated the sacraments, but his mind was frequently in turmoil.

Two years earlier when he had sailed to America, his ship, a small sailing vessel called the *Simmonds*, had run into a very bad gale and Wesley had been terrified of losing his life. And that terrified fear had made him realize that his faith was not as it should be. He was particularly struck by the behaviour of a group of Moravians – German Protestants – on board, who seemed to be serene and calm and to have a faith which he lacked. He determined to find out what it was that enabled them to stay so calm even in the face of a terrifying storm. The first thing he learned was that the Moravians spoke only one language, German. So Wesley began to teach himself German with the Moravians. He had a gift for languages and by the time he stepped off the ship in Georgia, he could speak German fluently.

On his return to England, he resigned from the missionary society. Three months later, on Wednesday, 24 May 1738, back in London, he was still searching for an assurance of faith. That night he attended a meeting in Aldersgate Street where someone was reading Martin Luther's preface to the letter to the Romans, and during the reading something happened to John Wesley. He wrote in his journal, 'I felt my heart strangely warmed . . . I felt that I did trust in Christ alone . . . that he had taken away *my* sins, even *mine*.' This was the day to which, for the rest of his life, he could look back and say, 'On that day – I *knew* – I was in the presence of Christ and I felt his forgiving, healing love.'

Of course, it doesn't happen for everybody in a blinding flash; sometimes it's a slow, gentle realization, a moment of insight, a moment of peace, perhaps sitting under a tree or standing by a river. A moment when we have a feeling of being at peace with the world and at one with God.

Then, in other times when the going is rough, it can help to look back and remind oneself of that moment of peaceful assurance, that moment when we *knew* that, in the end, in the words of Mother Julian of Norwich, 'All shall be well, and all shall be well, and all manner of things shall be well.'

> *Lord,*
> *when life is hard and the going rough*
> *remind us that your stillness and love*
> *are at the heart of every storm,*
> *and give us peace.*
> *Amen.*

Bread, holy and commonplace

I remember visiting an elderly man who was house-bound and asking him if he would like me to celebrate Holy Communion with him and his wife in his home. He thanked me but said there was no need because he and he wife had a practice of making ordinary meals special by blessing the food as if they were at Holy Communion. 'I hope that doesn't bother you,' he said. 'After all, all food is sacred, all bread is holy, isn't it? Wherever you eat it.'

He was right, of course: the ordinary things of life are holy. My wife and I once bought a rather nice set of pottery bowls from a lady potter in Canterbury. They were beautiful bowls, unusually delicate for pottery and a lovely colour. Some years later, when our set had suffered the occasional breakage, we went back to the pottery in Canterbury to ask for some re-placement bowls. It was a young man who greeted us this time, and when we described the bowls he knew them at once, 'Oh, yes,' he said, 'they were made by my mother. I'm afraid she died last year. I can make you something very similar, same colour, shape and size, but it won't be as delicate as my mother's work.'

So now we have 'mother' and 'son' bowls, and the difference is recognizable in the feel of them. One was made by a delicate hand, and the other is less delicate. They look similar, virtually identical, but they have a quite distinctive feel. I could tell you which one was 'mother' and which 'son' by feel, in the dark and blindfolded.

I like practical things to remind me of people I know or have known. We have a fretwork bookcase in daily use that was made over 100 years ago by my wife's grandfather when he was an apprentice. His task was to make a bookcase without the use of nails, screws or glue. I also have a useful box made by my father. And there is a kitchen knife with a wooden handle made by my father-in-law.

All these things – bowls, bookcase, box and kitchen knife – bring these people to mind whenever we use them, or touch them or see them. Through them we are, so to speak 'in communion' with people we have known and loved, they are with us in spirit. This is probably why Jesus chose commonplace things to remind us of him: bread and wine.

The man I visited was right about making every meal holy. Jesus said that we are to remember him whenever we break bread, and most of us do that several times a day. If we were to follow the example of my friend, then we would be aware of the presence of Jesus, and be 'in communion' with him every time we do it. That is an inspiring thought, but it is comforting too.

> *Loving God, who through the breaking of bread has given us a perpetual means of awareness of the presence of your Son, grant that, through the prompting of your Holy Spirit we may, each day, enjoy a living experience of the risen Christ, our Lord and Saviour.*
> *Amen.*

Casting stones

When I was a small boy there was a man who used to walk up and down the Pier Head in Liverpool wearing a sandwich board, which said on one side: 'Be sure your sins will find you out'. This used to worry me. 'Does this mean that my mother will find out that I've licked the jam knife?' (Knife-licking was forbidden – *absolutely*!) These things weigh heavily on your mind when you're six years old. Of course, nowadays you could rewrite the text to read: 'If you ever go into public life be sure the *newspapers* will find you out'.

Whether you are a bishop who made a mistake a quarter of a century ago, or whether you are acknowledged to be one of the legendary heroes or saints of the age, like Nelson Mandela or Archbishop Desmond Tutu, if you have done something as human as falling in love, having rows or making errors of judgement, you may be sure that the media will make the most of it. There is nothing more attractive to a news editor than a fallen idol.

I saw a programme on TV about Dr Albert Schweitzer, who built and ran a hospital in an equatorial African jungle for more than 40 years. The programme voiced criticisms of Albert Schweitzer, implying that he was a colonialist, and that his approach to Africans would now certainly fall short of modern, political correctness.

For heaven's sake! The man was born in 1875! He could have made a fortune in any career he chose. He was a world-famous organist. He wrote a book, still considered a classic, on Bach. He was a university professor, had a degree in Theology and was a qualified surgeon – but he chose to spend his life nursing the sick in equatorial Africa.

As evidence of his flawed character, a woman in the television programme said, 'In the end he became quite vain, you know. When the press photographers came, sometimes he would even put on a jacket!' Good heavens! Did the man have no shame?

When Jesus Christ was asked to judge someone's fall from grace he said, 'Let the one without sin cast the first stone.' I suppose I should be grateful that I am not employed to be a professional stone-thrower, though, come to think of it, I've just heaved a rather large brick at news editors. But there we are, nobody's perfect.

> *Lord,*
> *in the knowledge of my own shortcomings,*
> *let me not judge anyone in the light of*
> *   anything less*
> *than the light of your love.*
> *Amen.*

Change for the better

I was at a meeting of an organization which was discussing proposals for a new approach to its work. Of course, the very idea of 'new' approaches implies that old ways are likely to change. And it is amazing how resistant some people are to change. Throughout this meeting there was a continuous stream of negative and cynical comments, largely from just one person. He knew everything. He'd tried this, done that, been there and seen it all before.

The trouble with 'knowing everything' is that there is nothing left to learn, and the worldly-wise are inclined to have fixed ideas about the ways of the world. They believe that you can't actually change anything. Voting at parliamentary elections, for instance, is a waste of time, says the cynical 'know all', because all politicians, of whatever party, are basically 'out for themselves'. However, sometimes, just a few dedicated people can bring about huge amounts of change.

For instance, it is not all that long ago since the leaders of the most powerful governments in the western world met in Birmingham. The question of cancelling the debts of poor countries was not even on the agenda for discussion. When the idea was brought to their attention, the first response of the western world leaders was, 'It's all very complicated, and far too complex for the ordinary person to understand;

sadly, the idea of just cancelling the debts of the poor is just too simplistic.' It was pointed out to them that some poor countries had repaid the original debt over and over again, but they were so poor that they could never afford to pay back any of the capital. All they did do was to keep paying the interest; in some cases they had paid back nine times the original aid that had been given them. In other words, for every one pound we contributed to the poor countries, they gave us back nine – and we called this 'aid'.

More recently, the subject of third world debt *was* on the G8 agenda and $100 billion dollars of debt was cancelled. In terms of the Third World this was only a start, but at least it *was* a start. And it came about because a handful of dedicated people, who called themselves 'Jubilee 2000', campaigned to cancel the unpayable debts of the poorest countries in the world. This small group caught the compassionate imagination of thousands of ordinary people who believed that this unacceptable situation had to be changed. The problems of the Third World are still with us; millions of people are still dying of hunger and the rich western world is still exploiting undeveloped countries, but at least the problem is now on the agenda.

No matter what the cynical may say, I am convinced that we can all make a contribution to world peace and harmony. I believe that every good deed, every act of kindness, every gesture of love, no matter how small, can change the world. So if you are debating whether or not to do something kind or generous, debate no longer, do it, and you might tip the scales in favour of generosity and goodness far more than you could ever imagine.

Lord,
in the knowledge that even a glass of water
    given in your name
changes the world for the better, help us in
    small ways
to make a big difference, for your love's
    sake.
Amen.

Changing the world

Some years ago I was talking to a retired widower who kept saying things like 'I wish I'd learned to dance', or 'I've always envied people who could speak another language'; then he said, 'And that's another thing, I wish I'd learned to draw or paint. I really fancy doing that.'

So I said, 'Well, why don't you? There are all kinds of courses, night schools, adult education classes.' He looked at me as if I was saying something utterly ridiculous. 'I couldn't start doing all that kind of thing at my age.' In the end, however, he did go to a painting class and later he told me it was the best thing he had ever done.

In the 1960s I came across a book that was both funny and at times wise. It was called *How to live with yourself – or what to do until the psychiatrist comes*. It was written by a psychiatrist called Dr Murray Banks. One of the stories in his book was about a patient who had told him that the thing he most regretted in his life was not going to medical school to train as a doctor. He had achieved all the qualifications required to study medicine but there had been so many family crises he had never made it to college. The psychiatrist had asked the man, 'Why don't you go now?' and the man had said, 'Because it would take me seven years to complete the training and by the time I'd qualified, I'd be 47 years old.' The psychiatrist thought about this for a moment and then asked him, 'And in seven years, how old will you be if you don't go to medical school?' Happily the penny dropped and the man applied and was accepted to complete his studies.

I can't tell you how often I have heard people talk about 'not having the time', or 'being too busy', or 'I wouldn't know what to say or do'. So often people look at a task and it seems to take on 'impossible' proportions: 'it's all too much'; 'it's beyond me'. 'The world is in a terrible state, but what can I do about it?'

When I was a probationer minister, I made similar comments about the hopelessness of my job, the size and the impossible nature of the task, when a friend and colleague, a very experienced minister, said to me, 'If you make one sacrifice for the benefit of one other person, you will have changed the world for ever, and for the better: if you make two, that will be a hundred per cent improvement on your previous contribution. You're a young man, you've got 30 or 40 years ahead of you, so stop moaning and get cracking!'

Well, I haven't tried to keep a score, but it's a thought worth holding on to.

> Lord, help us to see that
> every sacrifice, every gesture of love,
> seen or unseen, however small,
> changes the world, and us, forever.
> Amen.

Christmas expectations

Christmas always seems to creep up on you. 'This year,' you vow in the autumn when supermarkets are playing their first Christmas carols, 'I really will prepare for Christmas in good time.' But the weeks rush by as you struggle to carry out your plans, and suddenly it's Christmas and Uncle Charlie and Auntie Jean are on the doorstep with their four little darlings and the puppy they couldn't keep secret till Christmas Day . . . One minute Christmas seemed ages away and suddenly, you're surrounded by wrapping paper and stuffed with mince pies and turkey.

Attitudes to the Christmas season vary somewhat. There is one which says, 'It's all commercialized rubbish, fairy lights, glitter, overeating and drinking too much.' Another says, 'Well, it's a lot of bother but it's for the children really, isn't it?' In some ways these are only minor variations of the views held by the characters in Charles Dickens' story, 'A Christmas Carol', in which Mr Scrooge declares:

'Bah! Humbug! . . . If I could work my will every idiot who goes about with 'Merry Christmas' on his lips, should be boiled with his own pudding, and buried with a stake of holly through his heart. He should!'

Scrooge's expectations were mean and miserly, but his nephew argued against him:

'[Christmas] is a good time; a kind, forgiving, charitable, pleasant time: the only time I know of, in the long calendar of the year, when men and women seem by one consent to open their shut-up hearts freely . . . and I say, God bless it!'

His sentiment is echoed, in all innocence, by the character Bob Cratchit's little boy, Tiny Tim, who offers a Christmas toast: 'God bless us, every one!'

Apparently, Dickens based his story on an earlier one he had written about a people-hating church sexton called Gabriel Grubb, who is carried off by goblins and, through a series of visions, is transformed into someone who loves his fellow human beings. Grubb had visions and Scrooge had dreams, but perhaps they were both, in some way, the self-fulfilling dreams and visions of Charles Dickens himself. He wrote to a friend about how, when he was writing this story, he had 'wept and laughed and then wept again . . . and walked the black streets of London many a night when sober folks had gone to bed'.

Was the story about himself? About his own discovery of the love that comes down at Christmas? Certainly the writing of the story had a marked effect on him, personally. When he finished it, he wrote to the same friend: 'I broke out like a madman . . . Such dinings, such dancings, such conjurings, such blindman's Bluffings . . . And if you could have seen me at a children's party the other night . . .'.

There is a saying, 'Be careful what you wish for, because it might come true'. But can someone wishing to be transformed into someone who loves their fellow human beings be a bad thing? And does that mean that deep down, beneath all that, 'Bah! Humbug!' Scrooge really wants to love and be loved?

Perhaps the real secret of Christmas is that it's not just 'for the children', nor is it simply the season for over-indulgence, but rather it's about, well, 'Love, actually'. So yes, we probably will eat too much, and spend too much on the children, but perhaps as well as all this, on Christmas Day we will remember the child in the stable, the love that came down at Christmas, and from the bottom of our hearts we will offer the toast, 'God bless us, every one', and pray for peace and goodwill throughout the world.

> *Lord of galaxy and space, whose incarnate*
>   *story*
> *enfolds astronomers, motherhood, poverty*
>   *and glory;*
> *weave your love within our hearts, that all*
>   *our fitful stops and starts*
> *may, as myrrh and frankincense, ascend as*
>   *prayer,*
> *that even our short stories might unfold*
> *facets of love, as lustrous still as Magi's*
>   *gold.*
> *Amen.*

Christmas journeys

Flicking through a batch of Christmas cards recently, it became clear to me that a great deal of travelling goes on at Christmas. Of course, the people who are going abroad for the festive season send their cards very early. We once received a card in October which read, 'We shall be in Spain this Christmas'. We have had cards from people spending their Christmas in South Africa, and from someone off to celebrate in Majorca. Now, I know it doesn't have quite the same exotic ring to it but my wife and I will travel all of 20 miles from our cottage in the Forest of Dean, with our daughter and her family from another cottage in the same village, to Gloucester to meet and celebrate with both the Gloucestershire branch and the Oxfordshire contingent of our family. And we will all bed down somehow, in both convenient and inconvenient places, happy in the knowledge that we will be celebrating Christmas together.

Dashing about at Christmas is all part of the fun, though I do have one particular plea to Christmas travellers on trains. Do you think we could cut down the use of our mobile phones? A train journey used to be a quiet, romantic escape, but now, our journeys are blighted by endless bleepings and voices shouting, 'Just pulling out of Basingstoke, darling! What? Sorry, you're breaking up!' Or worse, someone sharing their travel arrangements for the week followed by a report of the paper-clip situation in the Brighton office. Mobile phones, like credit cards, are wonderful, providing you never actually use them.

The Christmas story itself is about a family travelling a long way from home and having to bed down in an inconvenient place. It's the story of a child being born in a primitive environment, the story of a family who, like refugees, had to flee from a tyrant, King Herod; but it is above all a love story. It's the story of God's love for the human race – revealed in the innocence of a child. It's a story which says that tyrants may come and go – but the love that came down at Christmas will never die.

Wherever we celebrate Christmas this year, it must surely be the wish of every sane and rational person that we might create a world in which love, and not the tyrant, rules. So, in all your travelling, remember the love that comes down at Christmas, and even if there is a one-sided mobile-phone conversation happening in the next seat, just smile, and say to yourself, 'Happy Christmas, everyone, wherever you are going and wherever you are.'

> *Lord, in all our journeys,*
> *when we are weary, strengthen us;*
> *when we are afraid, comfort us;*
> *when we are alone, remind us of your*
>   *presence;*
> *and when travelling is done,*
> *unite us with those we love and with you,*
> *life's beginning and journey's end.*
> *Amen.*

Christmas laughter

Do you know how sometimes, for no apparent reason, a face from the past suddenly leaps to the front of your mind? It happened to me the other day. The face belonged to someone I once knew, named Harry Williams. I can see his face now, see him, large and laughing. He'd written a book called *Tensions*, in which he talked about what he called 'mountain top' experiences, those moments when you feel lifted up and close to God.

It is different, of course, for different people, but we can all probably recall one or more special moments when we have felt at peace and close to God. Harry Williams said that he felt closest to God in laughter, real laughter. By 'real', he meant open-hearted laughter, when you throw back your head and laugh uninhibitedly, especially at yourself. On the other hand, laughter, he said, goes badly wrong when it's some form of superior sneer, or it's sarcastic, or a snigger or a titter at someone else's expense.

Many of my most memorable 'peak' moments have been at special meals, such as Christmas gatherings, when, with family and friends who know and trust each other, the laughter has been totally uninhibited. Harry said that laughter is 'the purest form of response to God's acceptance of us', because when we can laugh at ourselves it means we accept ourselves, and when it is with other people, we are accepting them. Laughing at ourselves means accepting ourselves as we are, it means laughing at our pretensions, our mistakes, our failures, and it means forgiving ourselves; or, if you are laughing with someone else, forgiving and accepting them.

I once made a list of people who made me laugh. I don't mean professional comedians, it was mainly a list of friends, and just reading the names makes me smile. I think Harry Williams was right: laughter does lift you onto a different spiritual plain, which is why it is good when people greet you with a smile. It is good to know people whose laughter lives in your memory, and it is always good to be with people who can see the funny side of things.

Angels feature in the story of the nativity, as heavenly messengers. I wrote once about a Christmas shepherd whose vision of the first Christmas also included seeing the stars as laughing, singing, heavenly messengers:

> *Any shepherd worth his salt can sing the*
>   *night sky.*
> *Each star sounds a different note, a*
>   *different depth,*
> *and if you have ears, the night is loud with*
>   *stars,*
> *stars that cascade with laughter, are lyrical*
>   *with light,*
> *rippling, sparkling, dancing,*
> *for all the world like old friends*
> *holding lanterns and singing songs*
> *that cannot be heard in synagogue or*
>   *temple*
> *but thrill the ears of the throngs of heaven.*

I am convinced that there will be a lot of laughter in heaven. Jesus was born into a world that was full of wickedness and appalling violence, during the dark days of a military occupation, and yet, there was, I believe, laughter in the stable and in the air above Bethlehem when the heavenly hosts shouted for joy to celebrate the birth of the Son of God.

> *Dear loving, weeping, laughing Lord, may the timeless 'peace on earth' enjoyed by Mary and Joseph, shepherds and wise men, at that first Christmas, be experienced by all this Christmas, and may the happiness that comes 'gift-wrapped' in the love revealed in the manger child bring warmth and laughter and real 'joy' to everyone.*
> *Amen.*

Coded, wordless and private

A tutor at college once told us that if we felt hurt or angry about someone, it could be a very therapeutic exercise to sit down and write a full, frank, 'no punches pulled' letter to that particular person. It would do us the world of good, *providing*, we *never* posted the letter. 'This kind of letter,' he said, is written entirely for your own benefit, in fact, it would be better if it were written in code.'

When writing something that nobody else is ever likely to read, you don't have to worry about how well written it is. You can just let the words tumble out in any old higgledy-piggledy order. You don't have to worry about style, grammar or spelling, you just let it all fall out on the page, and your own incoherent rambling might make a kind of code of its own.

Curiously enough, as a writer, I have found frequently that when I just let my thoughts tumble onto the page, it can make far more interesting reading than when I am meticulously careful about the way I write. There's a kind of raw vitality about it, an unsophisticated, 'honest-to-God' expression of how I'm feeling.

In fact, if you want to do a little spiritual 'spring cleaning', writing down how you feel is a good way to go about it. Somehow, putting things down on paper helps to focus your thoughts. At those times when you seem to have so many problems you don't know where to begin, writing things down can help to sort them out. For instance, if you try to make a list of the things that are really bothering you, you are quite likely to find that there are really only one or two major problems that are the cause of all your other worries, and making a list can clarify the situation.

Many people who keep 'journals', or attempt to write a detailed account of each day in their diaries, often find that writing it all down is the first step to resolving a troublesome issue. There have been some very famous and notable diarists, thinkers, philosophers and politicians, from Samuel Pepys to Tony Benn. Samuel Pepys and John Wesley did take the precaution of writing in code, a kind of shorthand that only they could decipher. It was quite some time after their deaths before either of their codes were cracked.

People who find praying difficult might sometimes find it easier to write 'a letter to God'. Pouring out your soul to God on paper is a spiritually therapeutic thing to do, and it wouldn't really matter if you did it in some kind of code. After all, the one person who could see through your 'code' immediately would be God.

So, if someone, or something, is troubling you, try writing a full, frank and 'honest-to-God' letter about it. It will make you feel a lot better, but remember, don't post it unless it is addressed to the Almighty, in which case the letter will have been received and understood some considerable time before you wrote it.

Loving God, Father and Mother of us all,
we, your children, so often fail to find the
   right words,
or even any words,
to express our deepest feelings;
perhaps because we do not understand
   ourselves,
the people about us, or the world in which
   we live.
But your Holy Spirit hears even those
   groans
that are too deep for words, and interprets
   them
with love and generosity;
and in your mercy, we are blessed,
released from words
and able to rest in silence, in peace, and in
   you.
Amen.

Colours

The book of Genesis tells us that the patriach Israel loved his son Joseph so much that he made him a coat of many colours. The many-coloured coat was an expression of love; in fact, it was such a colourful expression of love that it filled Joseph's brothers with envy.

We frequently associate colours with emotional states. We talk of people being 'green with envy', or being 'red with rage', or so sad that they are 'blue'. People in a brooding, introspective state of mind are said to be in a 'brown study'. In heraldry black or sable is used to denote wisdom, prudence and constancy. In medieval Christian art yellow is the colour of Judas Iscariot's garments because yellow was associated with betrayal and cowardice.

For centuries the Church has used liturgical colours to represent religious ideas: purple for the penitential seasons of Advent and Lent, red for feasts of the Holy Spirit and of martyrs, white and gold for Eastertide, and green, the everyday colour of field and forest, for the 'Sundays in Ordinary Time'.

I once had a conversation with a man who told me that all his life he had seen auras of colour around people. The colours, he said, changed according to people's health and well-being. For many years he had assumed that everyone saw these 'auras', because he had always seen them. It was only as an adult that he gradually realized that other people did not see what he saw.

He told me that a mutual friend, who had just left the room, despite an outward show of normality, was deeply depressed. His 'aura' at that moment, he said, was a very deep purple. I knew that the person concerned was going through a very difficult time in his marriage, though the man who saw auras could not possibly have known this.

The colours he associated with anger, jealousy or distress were usually very stark and vibrant, whereas moods of love, laughter and spirituality were usually gentle, pale, pastel colours, sky blues and gold. I had, and still have, no reason to doubt this man's word. He was an extremely rational and modest man.

The idea that moods and emotions like anger and love have colours is a fascinating thought. Perhaps it might explain why some years earlier I had written a prayer that embraces a very similar idea:

> *Lord, let me reflect the colours of your*
> *   love;*
> *let my life be bright with laughter,*
> *my speech gentle,*
> *my thinking warm,*
> *my actions kind.*
> *And may all I suffer or enjoy,*
> *in the spectrum of my days,*
> *mellow and blend*
> *in peace and love and praise.*
> *Amen.*

Darkness, light and sight

There is a fascinating story in the Gospel of Mark when Jesus and his disciples are in the village of Bethsaida. A blind man is brought to Jesus and his friends beg Jesus to touch him. Jesus does so. He places his hands on the man's eyes and then asks him, 'Can you see anything?' The man opens his eyes and says, 'Yes. I can see people, but they look like trees walking about.' So Jesus places his hands on the man's eyes again, and when he takes his hands away, the man's eyesight returns completely and he can see clearly.

Remarkably, from an ophthalmic point of view, this story matches a modern, scientific understanding of how our eyes work. At first the man could not see properly but eventually, in two separate stages, his sight was restored. It was as if he had to learn gradually how to see, in the same way as a very young baby does. Our eyes are made so that a tiny picture of whatever is before us is formed on the light-sensitive screen at the back of the eyeball. This tiny picture (about two centimetres across and, incidentally, upside-down) is then sent by nerve fibres to the brain, which, in time, the new-born child sorts out and interprets the right way up.

You might also say that we need to learn how to 'see' spiritually. Even when people are dramatically 'converted' they don't see everything in a 'blinding flash'. The nature of a blinding flash is that it blinds you, at least temporarily. St Paul's spiritual journey led him onto the road to Damascus, where a flash of insight quite literally 'blinded' him. Gradually, his sight returned as his spiritual perception sharpened, as he learned how to 'focus' spiritually, through his encounter with the risen Christ.

When the 'eye of faith' is first opened, it does not see everything clearly, or immediately. The journey of faith is a learning process; we grow, in faith, step by step. As St Paul was to prophesy about eternity: 'Now, we see through a glass, darkly; but then face to face' (1 Cor. 13.12, KJV).

When we start out on our spiritual pilgrimage, there are many areas that remain, as it were, in the dark. As we grow in faith, our spiritual focus sharpens. We may possibly believe in fewer things than we did as children, but when we learn to focus, the essence of faith, the things of the spirit, are seen with greater clarity.

> *Heavenly Father,*
> *by whose grace we have been called*
> *out of darkness into your marvellous light;*
> *open our eyes to see your purpose for our*
>   *lives*
> *and help us to grow daily in faith*
> *and in the knowledge of your love.*
> *Amen.*

Discipline

When I was a probationer minister, not yet ordained, but working as a chaplain in a university and coming to terms with a new way of life, I had all the enthusiasm of a new disciple. But I was also beginning to understand what my college principal had meant when he had said in a lecture, 'You cannot be disciples without discipline.' About that time, I remember reading a passage by a writer called Harry Fosdick:

> No horse pulls a plough until it is harnessed. No steam or gas can drive an engine until it is confined. No waterfall can turn a turbo until the water is channelled. And no human hope can grow into achievement until it is focused and disciplined.

Discipline is not an attractive word; it sounds hard and difficult. It has several meanings. A discipline is a branch of learning, and a disciple is someone who is learning, or who is a follower of a particular school of thought or particular person. Discipline can also mean keeping something under control, such as a group of children in a classroom. The disciples of John Wesley were nicknamed the 'Methodists' because of their disciplined lifestyle and their approach to prayer and Bible study. Reading about them, I have found it rather ironic when people have dismissed religion as mere 'sentimental comfort for the feeble-minded'.

When I was a boy my mother gave me a book, a great spiritual classic by Thomas à Kempis, called *The Imitation of Christ*. Very few people achieve lives which are 'imitations' of Christ. To commit yourself to a Christ-like love and life is beyond most of us – to love your enemy, to turn the other cheek, to go the extra mile is never easy. In the film *Gandhi*, there is a moment when Gandhi is walking down a street in South Africa with a Christian clergyman. It looks as if they are about to be attacked by a gang of muggers, and Gandhi reminds the clergyman, with a smile, of Jesus' instruction to 'turn the other cheek'. The clergyman says, 'Oh, I don't think he meant it literally, I think he was speaking metaphorically.' 'Oh no,' replies Gandhi, 'I think he meant what he said.' It was Gandhi who, in later years, changed the history in India by getting his fellow-countrymen to do exactly that, to 'turn the other cheek'.

It is easy to talk about the theory and philosophy of Christianity; it is quite another thing to live by it. Jesus Christ's 'discipline' is the discipline of sacrificial love. It is a commitment to living by spiritual values rather than material; a commitment to the needs of the poor, the hungry and the homeless; a commitment to the love of God and our neighbour. It is not a sentimental, comfort-seeking flight from reality, but the very opposite. It is the demanding call to find real life by dying to self and living for others.

> *Lord, you call us to be disciples,*
> *teach us the discipleship of love;*
> *may our eyes be open to your truth,*
> *our ears alert to your call,*
> *and our feet ready to follow*
> *wherever you lead,*
> *for your love's sake.*
> *Amen.*

Doing good

I know that the expression 'do-gooder' is used as a term of cynical derision nowadays, but it was the term used by the apostle Peter to describe the life of Jesus. Peter was a fisherman, a plain, straightforward working man, not an orator or a politician, a poet or writer, and when he tried to describe the life of Jesus he did it in very down-to-earth language. He said of Jesus, quite simply, 'He went about doing good.'

A lot of people, in the newspapers, on television, on radio and, indeed, most of us as we go about our everyday lives, *talk* about the needs of the world, *argue* about injustice, poverty and hunger, but rarely find ourselves involved in *doing* anything, in practical terms, about the needs of the world or even our immediate community.

My mother used to have some rather curious sayings that puzzled me when I was a child. One of them was: 'Oh, him! He was going to break eggs with a big stick.' One day when she said it, I asked her, 'What do you *mean*, Mother? "He was going to break eggs with a big stick"?' 'Well,' she laughed, 'I mean – there's an awfully big difference between what he says he's going to do – and what he actually does.'

Jesus 'went about doing good'. Yes, he did talk and he did preach and teach, but it is amazing how much he taught by 'doing' rather than talking. He demonstrated his message by *doing* things. He healed the sick and the blind and the lame, and he got down on his knees and washed the feet of his disciples and then said to them, 'Do you see what I have done? Do you understand what I have done? I want you to serve and love each other as I have loved and served you.' On another occasion he said, 'I did not come to rule – but to serve. If you would be great – in my kingdom – you must be the *servant* of all.'

When people do devote themselves to serving, or 'doing good', like supporting an elderly person, or getting involved in a local attempt to meet the needs of the homeless, or offering to help as a volunteer in a hospice, it is never what they *say* that's impressive, so much as what they *do*.

It is in such loving and giving of ourselves, in our care for the poor, the sick or the dying that we see Christ living and loving in and through them. And through them, he is still 'going about and doing good'.

> *Lord Jesus,*
> *I give you my hands to do your work.*
> *I give you my feet to walk in your way.*
> *I give you my tongue to speak your word,*
> *and I give you my heart*
> *that through me*
> *you may love the Father*
> *and every human soul,*
> *today and always. Amen.*
>
> *Bishop Lancelot Andrewes (1555–1626)*

Don't worry about anything

One of the most common phrases in the English language is 'Don't worry', which is, of course, a lot easier to say than it is to do. In the New Testament, Jesus said, 'Can any of you by worrying add a single hour to your life?' (Matt. 6.27). St Paul, writing to the Philippians, says: 'Don't worry about anything, but in everything by prayer and supplication with thanksgiving let your requests be made known to God. And the peace of God, which surpasses all understanding, will guard your hearts and minds in Christ Jesus' (Phil. 4.6).

The fact is, we *do* become anxious. We become ill with anxiety, develop ulcers, have heart attacks, become deeply depressed. It was the awareness of people's anxieties that moved Chad Varah to found the Samaritans. The object was simply to befriend people in distress by listening.

I once met Chad Varah and I asked him how he would define anxiety. He said that anxiety is a *kind* of fear. We use the word 'fear' for something immediate and real, like someone pointing a gun at us, but we use anxiety for something which is not immediate and may not even *be* real. It may be something we're imagining, that isn't going to happen. And a lot of people become very anxious and almost incapacitated because of things which, if they could see them as they really are, would not make them so upset or worried.

Through his work with the Samaritans Chad Varah had learned that specific age groups had specific worries and anxieties. Youngsters worry about their attractiveness and the approval of their peers; students worry about their exams. People worry about their relationships with the people closest to them. The middle-aged worry about getting old. The old worry about taking care of themselves. Then there is anxiety about our health and, for everybody, anxiety about death, our own or that of someone close to us.

I asked Chad Varah what people could do about these very natural anxieties. He replied, 'Share them. If you can find someone who is sympathetic and will listen patiently to your anxiety, this is a great comfort and often helps to get things into proportion, so you stop making mountains out of molehills.' The most important thing is not to be alone with your problem. Find someone you care about, and who cares about you, and share it with that person. If it's so acute that sharing doesn't help, then see your doctor, maybe even ring the Samaritans. That's what they are there for.

> *Lord, teach me to see*
> *when problems disappear,*
> *that I have been a hostage*
> *to little more than fear.*
> *Each and every moment*
> *let me live within your sight,*
> *where present joy abides*
> *and fear is put to flight.*
> *Amen.*

Facing the future

On the radio, I heard a man saying that the main difference between a robot and a human being is the fact that human beings are self-conscious, and aware of their own existence. But then he went on to argue that, for most of the time, the human body – its hands, feet, arms and legs and so on – acts automatically, or robotically, and that our self-awareness does not really occupy much of our time. Therefore, he thought that the next few years would see the development of computers with very human-like 'brains' .

Well, my hope for the future has very little to do with robot computer brains. One of the 'self-conscious' things a computer *can't* do is to hope. Hope is a yearning, a longing, an attitude. I suspect a computer with 'attitude' might prove to be a bit of a handful.

Any minister or priest, doctor or nurse can tell you that 'attitude' – positive or negative – can have a massive influence in determining whether or not the sick will recover or deteriorate. Hope seems, at times, to defy science; or perhaps it is part of the psychology of healing that faith, hope and love can precipitate a healing process whilst cynicism and bitterness and anger can delay it.

Some people despair of the human race ever finding a way of living together in harmony and peace, but we need to face the future with hope, the hope which I believe is at the heart of the Lord's Prayer: 'Your kingdom come, your will be done, *on earth* – as it is in heaven.'

This is the hope that enabled Martin Luther King to dream of a world in which children of every race, creed and culture would be able to live in harmony, that enabled him to declare, 'If I knew for certain that the world was going to end tomorrow, I'd plant an apple tree – today.' Now, that's what I call 'facing the future with hope'.

> *Why are you cast down, O my soul,*
> *and why are you disquieted within me?*
> *Hope in God; for I shall again praise him,*
> *my help and my God.*
>
> Ps. 42

Facts, only facts

The brilliance and extravagance of a starlit night always takes my breath away. It is amazing to think that the starlight we see now has taken so long to reach us that the star it came from originally has died or exploded; such is the vastness of space. A much-published scientist said recently, that we 'used' to be overawed by the mysteries of creation. We now know the secrets of the universe; the facts of science have the answers to everything. Anyone who believes in God believes in a fantasy. I must say his intellectual arrogance took my breath away. It brings to mind that wonderful passage in the book of Job, when the arrogance of the 'know it all' is challenged with the words: 'Where were you when I laid the foundation of the earth? Who determined its measurements – surely you know! . . . On what were its bases sunk, or who laid its cornerstone when the morning stars sang together and all the heavenly beings shouted for joy?' (Job 38.4–7).

There is a certain amount of humour in the mental image of a creature whose life span is shorter than the blink of an eye in eternity, who lives on a small planet in a particular solar system which is only one of many, in a universe so vast it cannot be envisaged; a creature who is, in terms of the universe, so small as to make a flea look gigantic, jumping up and down and shouting, 'I know the answer to it all!' I'm afraid I am always worried by 'absolutists' of any kind, scientific or religious. I suspect judgements about 'the meaning of life' that are confined to material facts alone, where there is no room for flights of imagination, no room for spirituality, inspiration or poetry.

Leonardo da Vinci was undoubtedly one of the greatest artists the world has ever known, perhaps one of the greatest minds. He was a painter, sculptor, architect, scientist and engineer. In the fifteenth century he made drawings of fantastical machines which must have seemed like science fiction to his contemporaries; they were flights of fancy that, in the distant twentieth century, were to be realized in fact. He wrote in his notebooks: 'The poet ranks far below the painter in the representation of visible things and far below the musician in that of invisible things.' His mind was never confined to ideas that could only be supported by 'facts'.

If life is only about material facts, if human love is simply one group of bio-chemicals reacting to another group of bio-chemicals, then love as we know it does not exist. If in the scientific world of 'facts only', there is no such thing as spirituality, then neither is there need for what we understand to be emotion or compassion. Well, if that were the case, even if it were proven true a thousand times over, I would not care if the world thought me unintelligent, I would prefer the 'fantasy' of spirituality; I would prefer to continue my exploration into the heart of love, which I believe is God.

When we look at the stars with the 'eye of faith', we do not see a universe empty of intelligent life, signifying nothing in all its vastness, instead, we see each star and planet as:

The splash of a sounding,
Attempting to measure
The depth of eternal love.

Almighty God,
in joyous imagination,
let us see the stars as lanterns
held by generations of people
singing songs of love
and lighting the universe.
Let us see, know and enjoy
the light of your love
which is always with us,
in and through Jesus Christ, our Lord
and 'Light of the World'.
Amen.

Fasting

When I was a student, a small group from my college went to stay at a Franciscan friary. We were offered the choice of being guests and observers or of becoming, as it were, 'temporary' Franciscans, living as members of the community. We thought we would probably learn most by following their rule in the community, but none of us had realized the significance of the season – it was Lent. In Lent, Franciscans fast, and I can tell you they took fasting much more seriously than any of us ever had before, or since. Without doubt it sharpened and clarified the cutting edge of one's thinking.

Fasting is a practice common to many faiths. In Jewish communities, Yom Kippur, the Hebrew name for 'The Day of Atonement', is the annual Jewish Fast Day, observed by strict abstinence from food. For Muslims, Ramadan, which occurs in the ninth month of the Muslim year, is a time for fasting from sunrise to sunset.

In the Christian Church the Lent fast originally lasted for only two days, but was later extended to 40 days to commemorate Jesus' time of fasting in the wilderness. Of course, fasting for that length of time did not mean complete abstinence from food, but it did mean a pretty frugal diet. John the Baptist apparently survived for some time on a diet of locusts and wild honey.

Traditionally, in the Christian Church, Friday throughout the year was considered a day of fasting and abstinence from meat; fish was eaten instead. Every Friday was kept as a weekly commemoration of the Passion of Christ. Throughout my childhood, my mother, a Liverpool Irish Catholic, was devoted to her 'First Friday' novenas, which meant going to Holy Communion on every first Friday of the month for nine consecutive months. It is a devotional discipline, and my mother observed it continuously. When she had finished one novena she would immediately start another. She also fasted. That didn't mean she ate no food, but in the morning she would eat nothing before receiving Holy Communion; she would eat frugally throughout the day and she would never eat meat on any Friday.

To many people 'fasting' sounds like a rather negative activity, but whether you are religious or not, it's quite a good thing to do, in moderation, from time to time. Opera singers and many actors will fast for several hours before a performance, as it seems to give them an 'edge'.

The discovery I made in the friary was that I had fasted not only from food but also from a number of other things, like the car and the telephone. I realized I could continue to do this; I could break from my daily rituals. I could 'abstain' from watching television, listening to the radio or reading newspapers. I could have a day of 'giving' rather than 'taking', of being positive instead of negative.

My other lasting discovery was the realization that whilst, for me 'feeling hungry' is part of an occasional, optional exercise, for millions of men, women and children, it is a brutal way of life and, ultimately, death. Perhaps I could translate my occasional spiritual 'giving' rather than 'taking' into something rather more regular and practical.

> *Lord, help me to fast and abstain from sin,*
> *from selfishness and self-indulgence.*
> *Sharpen my spiritual awareness*
> *and increase in me a hunger for your*
>   *presence,*
> *your healing and your forgiving and*
>   *reconciling love.*
> *Amen.*

Father and Mother of us all

Throughout the centuries, God has traditionally been considered masculine. There was a bit of a shindig a few years ago when the Methodist Church produced a service book in which one of the prayers referred to God as the 'Father and Mother of us all'.

Thinking about this more deeply, if you believe that God is a spirit, then the whole idea of gender, male or female, is really rather inappropriate. Our traditional and continuous reference to God as 'He' is an indication of how limited our understanding of God has been. Reducing the concept of God to the male gender tells us, I think, more about human nature than it does about God.

Christianity emerged out of Judaism; and the God of Israel was a sophisticated concept. Look at the book of Genesis and imagine the period of history when this concept of God was brought into being; when people lived in fear of a whole range of tribal gods of sun, moon, stars, fire and water, gods of the harvest and man-made idols. The sons and daughters of Abraham, however, developed the belief in God as a spirit, who could not be seen, who was without form and whose name was unutterable. The poetry at the beginning of the Bible captures this beautifully: 'In the beginning God created the heaven and the earth. And the earth was without form, and void; and darkness was upon the face of the deep. And the spirit of God moved upon the face of the waters' (Gen. 1.1–2). There is no reference to 'he' or 'she'; this is a God above human gender.

The story of the creation in the book of Genesis is both poetic and inspired, but it isn't always wise to take poetry, or the Bible, literally. The Bible is a library of books: poetry, saga, parables, the work of inspired people searching for a way of expressing and describing the unsearchable and the inexpressible. The writers of the Old Testament, in their attempts to describe the might and power of Almighty God, used masculine words associated with warriors and fierce, sword-wielding, muscle-bound men. They would have found it difficult to conceive of a God who was vulnerable, or a God who had feminine attributes and qualities associated with gentleness, nurturing and motherhood. The concepts were completely alien to them.

To this day there are very few people who conceive of power in terms of love. Yet a God without feminine qualities is necessarily a deficient concept. Making God male seems to me to fall short of that wonderful vision of God as a spirit, moving on the face of the deep, who simply cannot be contained by name, image or gender.

If the human race is made in the image of God, then humanity cannot have qualities or attributes that God does not have. If motherhood is a human attribute, it seems to me that motherhood must also be embraced in the nature of God. If that is so, to refer to God as the Father and Mother of us all seems to me to take our understanding of the nature of God a stage further, which must be a good thing.

67

Loving God, Father and Mother of us all;
we thank you for the extravagance of your
   love.
May we share the gifts we have been given
with our sisters and brothers throughout
   the world,
that we may be as one in that never-ending
   circle of love
which is your nature and your being.
Amen.

Finding treasure

I was delighted to read about the father and son in Yorkshire, who, with a metal detector, discovered a trove of Viking treasure said to be worth more than a million pounds. When asked how they felt about finding something worth so much money they replied, 'It doesn't matter how much it's worth. We don't want 'owt. If we'd found just one coin we would have been over the moon. What is amazing is to be touching something that no one else has touched for over a thousand years.' For them the experience was of greater importance than the monetary value of the find.

Every day thousands of people buy National Lottery tickets and dream of becoming millionaires. A friend of mine told me that in the last 10 years she and her husband had gained just over £5,000 because of the National Lottery. When I raised my eyebrows at her confession she smiled and said, 'We gained £5,000 not by doing the Lottery, but by *not* doing it. In fact, we've never bought a lottery ticket. If, each week, you were to save the average amount spent by people doing the Lottery, which is about £5.00, well, for two people over 10 years, that amounts to £5,000.'

The belief that money will solve all their problems lies behind people's dreams of wealth. The real question, however, is about the difference between spiritual and material treasure: the things that are really valuable and those that are not.

In the Old Testament story (1 Kings 3.1–15), God was pleased with King Solomon when, instead of asking for riches, territory or long life, he asked for something imperishable: wisdom and insight. In Matthew's Gospel too, the kingdom of God is described as a treasure found in a field, not in terms of material wealth but as something so valuable that you would give up everything else to possess it.

The writer Gerard Hughes once wrote about 'the treasure in the field': 'The treasure – is the love of God – and the field – is *you*.' This reminds me of another quote from the Old Testament about King Solomon. When he was about to start building the Temple in Jerusalem he prayed: 'But who is able to build [God] a house, since heaven, even highest heaven, cannot contain him?' (2 Chron. 2.6).

Years later St Paul was to write, 'Do you not know that you are God's temple, and that God's Spirit dwells in you?' (1 Cor. 3.16). This is, of course, what Gerard Hughes was saying when he said that 'you are the field'. The 'treasure' is the Spirit of God. And you are God's temple. You are the field in which God is hidden. Real treasure, the things of real value, are not material, but spiritual.

The wonder of the kingdom of God is that it is not dependent on perishable things like land, property or wealth, but on eternal things like love, joy, wisdom and peace.

Finding treasure

God of love, the source of life and meaning,
grant us humility to recognize our
      ignorance
and courage to seek your wisdom;
honesty to realize our weakness,
wisdom to find your strength
and the joy which comes
not from getting but from giving,
not from gaining material things
but from love and loving,
in the name of Jesus Christ, your Son.
Amen.

Forgiveness and healing

In the Lord's Prayer, there is one phrase that has a condition attached to it: 'Forgive us our sins as we forgive those who sin against us.'

It is, I think, significant that Jesus once healed a man by saying, 'Your sins are forgiven you.' Forgiveness is a means of healing: of relationships, of sinners, of people who have caused offence. But the person who offers forgiveness is often healed as much, if not more, as the one who is forgiven. Those who find it difficult or even impossible to forgive are burdened people. The heaviest load we ever carry is a massive grudge.

Francis of Assisi wrote, 'It is in giving that we receive; it is in pardoning that we are pardoned' and 'It is in dying that we are born to eternal life.' I think forgiveness is part of the essence of resurrection. I have seen people who were spiritually deadened by anger and hatred, people who spent years in a self-imposed limbo of bitterness because of their inability to forgive someone. And I have seen the same people come to life through the healing power of forgiveness.

'Father forgive them, they know not what they do.' This prayer was among the last words of Jesus Christ, and one of his last actions was to offer forgiveness and the promise of new life to the repentant thief on the cross next to his own: 'Today, you will be with me in Paradise.' Jesus' promise also revealed something of the nature of the forgiveness offered to those who turn to him. There is no waiting of any kind – no period of adjustment, no probationary period, '*Today* – you will be with me in Paradise.' When God forgives, it is immediate, and our sins are forgotten for ever.

Some years ago I talked on a television programme with the then Master of the Rolls, Lord Denning, about forgiveness and the law. He said that the law could be merciful, it could reprieve, it could show clemency and offer pardon when appropriate. But when I asked, 'Does the law ever erase the offence, treat the guilty person as if the offence had never been committed?' he said, 'Oh no. You're talking about divine forgiveness. Only divine forgiveness erases the offence; the law never forgets.'

John Wesley had an enormous capacity for forgiveness. Throughout a long life of being attacked by mobs and reviled even by fellow churchmen, he never held a grudge; whether the attacks had been physical or intellectual he always prayed for those who abused him. In the same spirit, let us pray for grace to forgive those who have offended us, for their spiritual health and happiness, that we might be reconciled to each other and to God.

> *Loving God, forgive us our sins as we forgive those who have sinned against us, and, seeing and acknowledging how much we have been forgiven, may we also forgive with the same generosity of spirit, for the sake of Jesus Christ our Lord.*
> *Amen.*

Freedom through forgiveness

There is a pub in Kent called 'The Three Chimneys'. It gained its name through a misunderstanding of a French phrase. During the Napoleonic Wars a number of French soldiers were imprisoned in Sissinghurst Castle. From time to time they were given leave to walk out of the castle, having given their word that they would not go beyond the parole limits, which in this case was no further than a junction of three roads, or 'the three ways', a mile or two away from the castle. The French phrase for 'the three ways' was 'les trois chemins' which Kentish ears translated into 'the three chimneys'.

During the Napoleonic Wars there were over 100,000 French prisoners all over England. Not long ago when I was reading the Journal of John Wesley, I came across this entry, written when Wesley was touring Cornwall:

Sunday, September 18th 1757:

At eight, many of the French prisoners were mixed with the usual congregation. This was doubled at one, but still came nothing near to that which assembled at Gwennap in the evening. It rained all the time I preached; but none went away, a shower of rain will not fright experienced soldiers.

Here I learnt of a remarkable occurrence. A few days ago, some hundred English, who had been prisoners in France, were landed at Penzance by a cartel ship. Many of these passed through Redruth, going home; but in a most forlorn condition. None showed more compassion to them than the French. They gave them food, clothes or money, and told them, 'We wish we could do more; but we have little for ourselves here.' Several who had only two shirts gave a naked Englishman one. A French boy meeting an English boy, who was half naked, took hold of him, and stopped him, cried over him a while, and then pulled off his own coat and put it upon him!

Jesus said, 'You have heard that it was said, "An eye for an eye and a tooth for a tooth". But I say to you, Love your enemies and pray for those who persecute you' (Matt. 5.43–44).

I heard recently of a nurse, imprisoned by the Japanese during the Second World War, who was asked what she felt now about her captors. She said 'Oh, I forgave the Japanese years ago. I had to. If I had not forgiven them, I would still be imprisoned by them even now, imprisoned by the anger and bitterness of those days. If you want to be really free – you have to forgive, in order to start a fresh life.'

Our freedom is in the forgiveness and love of others; our hope for eternity is in God's forgiveness and love of us.

Heavenly Father, you have taught us,
    through your Son,
that if we do not forgive others, we cannot
    receive forgiveness;
make us merciful in our dealings with
    those who do us wrong,
that we might be freed from the
    imprisonment of bitterness and anger,
for the sake of him who died that we might
    be forgiven,
even our Saviour, Jesus Christ.
Amen.

God helps those who . . .

It was from George Macleod, the founder of the Iona community in Scotland, that I heard a wonderful illustration of the saying 'God helps those who help themselves'. He told me a story of his namesake, a Church of Scotland minister, the Revd Dr Norman Macleod.

Apparently when Norman Macleod was a theological student in Edinburgh, he became a close friend of another student who was physically his opposite. Norman Macleod was a very big man, tall, broad and strong; he would not have been out of place at the Highland Games. His friend, on the other hand, was a small, thin, frail-looking man. Nevertheless, they had much in common in their theological thinking.

As students, in the summer vacations they went on fishing trips on the West Coast, from Oban. In later life, the big man and the little man and their wives used to holiday together. They would hire a boat and a boatman to take them out to do a little offshore fishing.

One year the four of them had put out from Oban, in a big open boat, with a weathered local fisherman at the oars. They were perhaps about a mile offshore when the weather quite suddenly took a change for the worse – a brooding squall cloud began to darken the sky and the boatman said, in the beautifully precise and sibilant accent of the Scottish Highlands, 'Ay, ladies and gentlemen, I am afraid – I have to tell you – that we must beat for the shore. But I also have to tell you – that, ay, we will not make it.'

Big Norman Macleod turned towards the boatman. He laid his huge hand on the boatman's arm. 'What do you mean, man, we won't make it?'

'I mean, sir, that we will not make it to the shore before *that*,' and he pointed to the squall cloud, 'catches up wi' us!'

Not surprisingly there was consternation in the boat. Then Norman Macleod's lifelong friend, looking somewhat smaller and frailer than usual, turned to the ladies and said: 'Ladies, should we ask Dr Macleod to lead us in prayer?'

The ladies thought this was a very good idea, but the boatman disagreed, with some vigour: 'Och, no, no, no, – away with you! Let the *wee* mannie pray – and let the big one tak' an oar!'

Too often we expect God to do it all for us when, in fact, sometimes God answers our prayers by saying, 'I have given you gifts and graces, talents and strengths; use what I have given you to help yourself in this situation.'

Almighty God, you have blessed us with so many
  gifts and graces;
in your mercy teach us to use your gifts
that we might live and work to your praise and
  glory.
Amen.

Granny

I was watching a late-night movie recently, called *A Woman's Tale*, about a spirited old lady who resists her son's attempts to move her into a nursing home. Her refusal to give up her independence was both inspiring and life-affirming. A phrase she kept using was: 'Let's do a bit more living.'

I have seen several films with a similar theme, but what I liked about this one was that it avoided the sentimentality that usually accompanies such a subject. However, the question that all these films raises is 'What's happened to our concept of family in recent years?'

There are many wonderful cartoonists about these days but I have to confess to missing the late and much-lamented *GILES*. The character I liked most of all in these cartoons was 'Granny'. She may have been a bit difficult at times, but she was always part of that wonderful family, with Mum and Dad, sons and daughters and grandchildren of every conceivable shape and size. It didn't matter if they were having a picnic in a field, or clambering over a floating Gin Palace at the Earl's Court Boat Show, or sitting on the beach at Bournemouth, 'Gran' was always in the picture, an integral part of the family. She always had her hat on, and she was frequently doing the unex-pected, like reading the *Racing Times,* or checking her football pools.

I know there are all kinds of situations when an elderly parent has to have residential or nursing care, but I have an uncomfortable feeling that there are quite a few Grandmas and Grandpas in care homes simply because they are perceived as 'too demanding'. I remember a Victoria Wood sketch in which a character says, 'I'd love to have him at home, but I'm out all day and he might fall and break something – like a vase.'

Today there are insurance schemes designed to safeguard the homes of the elderly to provide funds for when they move into residential care. No doubt very wise. Personally, I think we should be looking for ways of making it more attractive for families to keep Granny at home. After all, one of the Ten Commandments is 'Honour your father and your mother' and that was written when the tribes of Israel probably took their grannies everywhere.

> *O Lord, support us all the day long of this*
> *troublous life*
> *until the shades lengthen and the evening*
> *comes,*
> *and the busy world is hushed, the fever of*
> *life is over, and our work is done.*
> *Then, Lord, in your mercy, grant us safe*
> *lodging, a holy rest,*
> *and peace at the last; through Jesus Christ*
> *our Lord.*
> *Amen.*
>
> *Cardinal John Henry Newman 1801–90*

Growing up

In 1942, when I was five, my best friend was Roy, and he had a sister called June. Roy's father was away from home because he was in the army in North Africa, and my father worked in Cammell Laird's shipyard in Liverpool, building submarines.

We grew up to the sound of air-raid sirens, the throbbing of German bombers and blasts and crashes in the night. It never worried us because when the war broke out we were only babies and we didn't know any other way of life. So in the morning we searched for interesting bits of shrapnel and made 'dens' among the rubble.

In the background of our lives were seagulls' cries and ships' fog-horns that sounded all day long as tugboats, cargo vessels, warships and ferry-boats manoeuvred in the River Mersey. Then there was the wireless, with its accumulator batteries, on which we heard the voice of Winston Churchill, laughed together at Tommy Handley and Jack Train in ITMA, and rushed home for *Dick Barton, Special Agent*. My father practised his bass trombone in the front room, and my mother sang music-hall songs in the back kitchen.

During the week I went to St Anne's School, Rock Ferry in Birkenhead where the primary teachers were

nuns. We were given Holy Pictures when we success-
fully recited the catechism, and on Sundays we went
to Mass, said or sung in Latin with an Irish accent.

Later, when I won a place at St Anselm's College
which served the Wirral and North Cheshire, I was
told that I came from a 'rough' area. It didn't seem
'rough' to me. It was full of laughing uncles and singing aunties. It was wonderful to me, but then we were
innocents, Roy and June and I. We didn't understand
the evil that caused and drove the war along. We
didn't understand death or know much about suffering, even though it must have been all around us.
There was a war going on over our heads and in our
streets, but we were protected by our innocence. Roy,
June and I lived in our own safe little world, the world
of children's imagination.

Perhaps that's what heaven really is: the recaptur-
ing of innocence. Jesus said that unless we become
like children we will not enter the kingdom of heaven.
Perhaps Paradise is a place and a state of mind and
being where evil isn't even imagined or thought of,
where innocence and laughter and music are enjoyed
as they were intended to be, to the glory of God.

> *Almighty God, as your beloved Son, Jesus,
> innocent of heart and mind, lived and died
> in an occupied country under military rule,
> yet taught the world the healing power of
> forgiveness and reconciliation, so fill our
> lives with your Holy Spirit, that innocence
> and love may reign in us, and in our world,
> for ever.*
> *Amen.*

Gunpowder, treason and . . . freedom?

'Remember, remember, the fifth of November, gunpowder, treason and plot!' This little rhyme, learned in childhood, reminds us of the infamous plot to blow up Parliament. We remember it on 5 November when we light bonfires and have firework displays. We know the name of Guy Fawkes, but we might find it more difficult to name the issue that drove the plotters to attempt such an extreme measure. In a word, or rather two words, the heart of the matter was 'religious freedom'. The men involved in the Gunpowder Plot were angry that, as Catholics, they had been promised religious freedom, but now the King, James I, had gone back on his word. They wanted the freedom to worship according to their consciences, to celebrate Mass or any Catholic religious service without the fear of arrest and imprisonment.

All this happened a long time ago in 1605, but some of the issues of that time still concern us today. Not long ago, I attended a conference on 'Freedom Through Faith'. We were a motley bunch of Anglicans, Methodists, Catholics, Baptists, United Reformed Church and Elim Pentecostals. We sang hymns together, debated, laughed, prayed and worshipped together – and perhaps it is worth remembering that this kind of religious freedom was won at a very high price. People were arrested, imprisoned, tortured and executed before that freedom was achieved.

We are a multicultural, multifaith society now, and in Britain, Christians, Jews, Muslims, Buddhists, Hindus all are free, in law, to practise their religion without restriction or fear of reprisal. Yet all around the world violent conflict continues and very often it appears to be based on religious and cultural differences.

At the 'Freedom through Faith' conference, the deeper we went in our search for the causes of religious intolerance the clearer it became that the real issues behind most of the world's conflicts, throughout history, were not religious but economic. International conflict, often dressed up as defending some religious issue, is revealed, under close inspection, to be about territorial claims or control of wealth.

Today, we frequently hear politicians talk about bringing democracy and freedom to other nations, when the real reason for military action and occupation of someone else's sovereign territory has very little to do with democracy and a lot to do with economics. We can only hope and pray for the day when God's will is done on earth as it is in heaven, and the only kingdom that matters is God's kingdom – where all people will be truly free.

> *Almighty God, we thank you for the many freedoms we enjoy and for those who have laboured to secure them. Give us grace to defend human liberty and to proclaim our convictions in such a way that all our work is seen to be in harmony with your nature revealed in Jesus to be one that embraces forgiveness, healing, reconciliation and love. Amen.*

Head to heart

Like many Christian churches, the Methodist Church of Great Britain has an annual conference. For Methodists, this is the chief council of their Church, the final arbiter of its doctrine and practice. The conference was founded by John Wesley who was an academic: a fellow of Lincoln College Oxford, equally at home with Latin, Greek, French or German; and a great theological debater. In some ways, it was his academic ability, his rational and intellectual approach to religion that prevented him, for some time, from becoming totally committed as a Christian believer.

He and his brother Charles had a very similar education at the same school and the same university. Both were ordained as priests in the Church of England, and both went to work with the early settlers of North America. Both struggled to come to terms with their Christian faith. Though they were very different personalities, they both experienced a spiritual life-changing experience within a few days of each other.

Charles was living in lodgings above a shop in Little Britain in London, owned by a Mr Bray, described by Charles as, 'a poor ignorant mechanic who knows nothing but Christ; yet by knowing him knows and discerns all things'. Charles was very ill with pleurisy and seemed to be getting worse. Mr Bray's sister, a Mrs Turner, was convinced in a dream that Jesus had spoken to her and told her to go to the clergyman staying in her brother's house. She told her brother that she believed that his lodger, the Reverend Mr Charles Wesley, was 'troubled in his soul'.

She was perplexed as to how to go about her task. She didn't have the nerve to enter into a discussion with such an educated man as Charles, but she felt she must do something. So she went up to the room where Charles was lying, knelt down outside the door and spoke to him through the keyhole. She said, 'In the name of Jesus Christ, arise and thou shall be healed of all thy infirmities.'

Mrs Turner's disembodied words, coming through the keyhole, changed Charles' life. They set off a train of thought that ended in his absolute conviction of the love of God for him, personally. From that moment he began to recover his health. All this happened on Pentecost Sunday, 21 May 1738, and a few days later, on 24 May, his brother John came to visit him to tell him that he had had a similar experience of God speaking to him through someone else's words, and how he had felt his heart, 'strangely warmed'.

At last, the Wesleys had made the leap from head to heart, from intellectual argument to an awareness of the presence of God and the realization that faith is not about *proving*, but about *entering into* a relationship based on love.

> *Lord, in your mercy,*
> *do not let our 'cleverness' create barriers*
> * between us.*
> *Help us, instead, to make the leap from*
> * head to heart,*
> *that our faith might grow in love.*
> *Amen.*

Healing and wholeness

From time to time I am asked if I believe in healing, and if there are people who have a healing gift. My immediate answer is yes, that I have been blessed by an experience of healing; but secondly I add that I some have reservations on the subject.

First, my experience of healers, that is people who have an actual healing gift, is that they are, generally, quiet people, not given to displays of loud and dramatic appeals to the Almighty. The healers I have met, whether the healing was in their voices or in their hands, administered both without drama or noise.

I suspect that in some healing services, when people shout and become excitable, even if healing is being administered, something else is going on as well. It might be about creating the conditions under which some people become more susceptible to suggestion. I don't know. But if we take Jesus as our example, he was himself a quiet healer. He did heal in public, but the accounts of those healings suggest calm and quiet.

Jesus offered people forgiveness, reconciliation and the love of God, all of which are factors in healing. At the heart of a great deal of illness is the inability to forgive or to accept forgiveness. The deep-seated need for reconciliation may be so well hidden and so deep that people are unaware of it, and ask for treatment only for the symptoms. We are aware that Jesus was concerned with wholeness, allowing people to fulfil their spiritual and emotional potential. Physical well-being is, of course, only a part of being 'whole'.

Inner healing is concerned with bringing to light the causes of the deep-rooted suffering of mind, body and soul. To help the sufferer understand and interpret the causes accurately and usefully, counselling and prayerful reflection is likely to be every bit as important as healing hands.

In the eighteenth century John Wesley published a book called *Primitive Physick, or an easy and natural way of curing most diseases*. It is full of advice about various illnesses and the medicines prescribed are, for the most part, herbal. Psychology was not developed as an academic subject until the late nineteenth century, but then, as an eminent psychologist, H. Ebbinghaus, has said, 'Psychology has a long past, but only a short history.' John Wesley who, as Dr Johnson observed, could 'talk well on any subject', understood quite a lot about the psychology of health, although his term for psychology was 'the passions', by which he meant people's emotional and mental condition. He considered, the 'passions' to be at the root of many if not most illnesses. In the Bible, the book of Proverbs says that a merry heart does good like a medicine, and it is true that humour and laughter and joy are also healing agents. So let's pray for wholeness of body, mind and spirit.

> *Forgiving, reconciling and healing God,*
> *we remember in your presence those who*
> *are ill.*

Healing and wholeness

Bless all that is being done for their good,
and surround all of us with your healing
love and power,
that your will may be done, on earth as it
is in heaven,
through Jesus Christ, our Lord and
Saviour.
Amen.

Hearing the call to do good

I read an article in a national newspaper in which the reviewer referred to John Wesley as a 'prig'. I would have been proud to have had such a 'prig' as a friend. Look at this extract from the journal of John Wesley, dated 4 January 1785. At this time he was in London and he was 82 years old:

> At this season we usually distribute coals and bread among the poor of the Society; but I now considered they wanted clothes as well as food; so on this and the four following days I walked through the town, and begged two hundred pounds, in order to clothe them that wanted it most; but it was hard work, as most of the streets were filled with melting snow, which often lay ankle deep, so that my feet were steeped in snow-water nearly from morning till evening.

During his lifetime through his 'begging'; he raised thousands of pounds for the poor. He also earned a great deal of money from publishing, but gave it away. In those days there was a tax on silver and the Revenue people did not believe that he had not earned any, so they wrote to him, demanding a declaration of all the silver he possessed. This was his reply:

Sir, I have two silver teaspoons at London
and two at Bristol. This is all the plate which
I have at present. And I shall not buy any
more while so many round me want bread.
I am, Sir, your most humble servant,
John Wesley

A prig is a narrow-minded, self-righteous person.
Wesley was never that. He was a brilliant public
speaker, a mimic with a great sense of humour. Here
is a letter he wrote to a woman who clearly has asked
him for money on several occasions:

Dear Patty,

You don't consider – money never stays with
me; it would burn me if it did. I throw it
out of my hands as soon as possible, lest it
should find a way into my heart. Therefore
you should have spoken to me while I was
in London, and before Miss Lewen's money
'flew' away. However, I know not but I
may still spare you five pounds, provided
you won't say, 'I will never ask you again',
because that is more than you can tell; and
you mustn't promise more than you can
perform.

This was a man who set up dispensaries giving free
medicines to the poor, who set up free schools and
founded homes for widows. Perhaps not a 'prig' then,
but certainly a 'do-gooder'. Funny isn't it, how some
people mock 'do-gooders'? Is it because they prick
our conscience? After all, you don't have to take any
notice of a man you can mock, do you? Perhaps Max
Beerbohm was right when he wrote, 'The Non-Con-
formist conscience makes cowards of us all.'

Loving God,
forgive me that I have so often found
  excuses
to resist hearing the call to service or
  sacrifice.
Our Lord Jesus Christ went about doing
  good
and died with the sound of mocking voices
  in his ears.
In your mercy, give me courage
to stand up and be counted,
and to find joy in serving you
for the sake of your kingdom.
Amen.

Hidden women

It came as a surprise to me to learn that the great explorer, David Livingstone, was usually accompanied on his expeditions into the African interior by his wife. In fact, it was Mrs Livingstone who organized the trips, made arrangements with the Africans and started the schools. She also managed to give birth to the Livingstone children at the same time. Thinking back, I don't think I was even aware that David Livingstone had a wife.

John Wesley was born, in 1703, into the midst of a great family of clergymen, yet if you were to search for the person who influenced him most, you would find that his greatest inspiration and guidance came from his mother, Susanna.

John was Susanna's fifteenth child, and she went on to have half-a-dozen more. Although some of her children did not survive infancy she still had a very large family to nurture. She educated all her children in her own kitchen schoolroom. Susanna was ahead of her time with regard to the education of girls; Number 8 on her list of rules said, 'That no girl be taught to work till she can read very well . . . putting children to learn *sewing* before they can *read* perfectly is the very reason why so few women can read to be heard, and never to be well understood.'

93

Susanna wrote prayers, meditations and theological papers to help the children to understand their faith. She set aside special times to talk to each of them individually. In 1732, this was her timetable: 'On Mondays I talk with Molly; on Tuesday, with Hetty; Wednesday, with Nancy; Thursday, with Jacky (that was John Wesley) Friday, with Patty; Saturday, with Charles; and with Emily and Sukey together, on Sunday.' Imagine the impression these private sessions must have made on those children. If John and Charles Wesley were the Fathers of Methodism, the 'Mother' of Methodism was surely Susanna.

I wonder how many other great women are hidden behind the great men of history. I suspect that through the centuries there have been thousands whose stories we may never know. In our prayers tonight, let us pray for all the unsung heroines of history, and the 'hidden' women of our own time.

> *Almighty God, we give you thanks for all those who have influenced, inspired and nurtured us, particularly our mothers, and for all those women who give, or have given, their time, talents and lives for the sake and for the love of others.*
> *Amen.*

Holy Week meditation

Praying before the Stations of the Cross is a very ancient devotional exercise, practised throughout the year, but it has special significance in Lent and Holy Week. There is evidence from a very early date that Christian pilgrims to Jerusalem made a practice of following the traditional route taken by Jesus from the house of the Roman Governor, Pontius Pilate, to Calvary and ultimately to the tomb in which Jesus was laid. As they made this journey they would stop and recall particular incidents in the Passion at various places along the route and pray and meditate on the sufferings of Christ.

Modern pilgrims find the Stations, carved in stone tablets, along the Via Dolorosa in the old city where the atmosphere seems hardly to have changed since biblical times. Every year, throughout Holy Week, hundreds of pilgrims walk in the steps of Jesus, praying at each of the Stations. One of them envisages, on that terrible walk, a meeting between Jesus and Mary, his mother:

> Mary did not speak,
> did not weep,
> did not touch,
> but they met.
>
> In the lane

from the Damascus Gate
dealers touted for custom,
money-changers eyed travellers,
assessing their worth, wary.

The air was thick with aromas,
spices, meat on spits,
animals and people,
and noise,
hooves and hammers
clanking, clinking,
clucking, bleating,
soldiers joking,
women shouting,
children laughing.

In the midst of babble
they met,
in a pocket
of love-charged silence.

All her life
she had searched for him,
the child she had held
but could not hold,
the elusive core of him
beyond her reach.
But now,
in one long look
the years compressed,
from cradle to Egypt,
from carpentry
to Hosannas on a donkey,
Simeon's sword sinking deeper
and yet
she was nearer to him now
than she had ever been.

Holy Week meditation

The mystery of his birth,
the mystery of his being
touched her, embraced her
into the mystery of his death.

When tears came
they did not reproach,
neither was there question
in her pain.

In the din
of money and men,
alone with him
her silence said,
'Behold, the handmaid of the Lord.'

Loving God,
in temptation's hour may we imitate
    Mary's obedience,
when truth is mocked may we possess her
    courage and loyalty,
and in the hour of trial, may we know the
    love she gazed upon at Calvary.
Amen.

I love, therefore I am

Some people define who they are in terms of what they are, or have become. 'I am a football manager'; 'I am a surgeon'; 'I am a teacher'; 'I have achieved this station in life, this role, and I exist at my best when I am fulfilling this role. In other words, I am what I do.'

Others feel they are defined by their 'public image', that is, what others think of them. One of the most insecure people I ever met was a successful actor, who believed that if he lost his popularity, his life would be over; he would cease to exist.

There are also those who measure themselves by the power they can wield through their wealth or, in other words, 'I am what I have in the bank.' A friend once told me of a cruise she went on, in which some very rich people were extremely rude and overbearing towards the stewards, maids, waiters and waitresses. They clearly believed that their wealth made them superior to other people. Of course, the world does seem to measure people in terms of financial success, or in terms of fame and fortune. In reality these are insubstantial things over which we do not have complete control – they can very easily slip away, or be taken from us.

Clearly it is a big mistake to define oneself in terms of 'external' things like money, property or status. What we *are*, who we are, deep down, depends on 'internal' spiritual things, like the depth of our compassion, our truthfulness, our ability to endure, our capacity for laughter and love: these are qualities that determine who we really are. The French philosopher, Descartes, famously declared, 'Cogito, ergo sum' – 'I think, therefore I am.' There are others, however, who think that is not enough.

Christians believe that our entire reason for existence is to love and to be loved, to love God, and to love our neighbour as ourselves. Therefore, I have meaning because I am someone who loves and is loved. Perhaps one could say, 'I love, therefore I am.' Some people believe that many of the world's problems spring from the idea that wealth and power are the keys to human happiness and fulfilment, when in fact the world was designed to function at its best under a rule of love, forgiveness and reconciliation.

There's a theory that says that the earth is a dormant paradise waiting to come back into life. But it can only function as a paradise when those who inhabit it are more concerned about serving rather than being served. In the paradise of the Garden of Eden, everything went wrong when the people in it began to say, 'Never mind what God wants, give me what I want.'

If we actually took the commandment to 'love one another' seriously, if 'love' was the chief rule of the human race, then there would be no wars, no racial prejudice, no ethnic cleansing, no pollution, no hungry, no homeless. But it's just a theory. It wouldn't work, would it? Or would it? Is there just a smidgeon of truth in G.K. Chesterton's saying that 'Christianity has not been tried and found wanting, it's been found difficult and not tried.'

Loving God, you sent your Son, Jesus Christ, into the world to teach us that your nature is love, to turn upside down the values of the world, to reveal that in the kingdom of God, in heaven and on earth, the first shall be last and the last first, and the highest rank is that of servant. Lord, may your Holy Spirit enable us to walk in the footsteps of Jesus, to live as he lived and love as he loved, so that your kingdom may come and your will be done, on earth as it is in heaven. Amen.

In service

Some years ago there was a popular television series called *Upstairs Downstairs*, which gave us an insight into the world of Victorian society, and showed us something of what it meant to be 'in service'. It was as much a trade or profession as any other form of employment. To work as a lady's maid, a footman or a butler in some great household was not seen as demeaning but as an honour. Being 'in service' had its roots in the 'age of chivalry'.

Centuries ago, a young boy might begin his education as a 'page' at the age of seven in the castle of a nobleman. Here, until he was 14, he served his Lord and Lady. It was his duty to wait on them at table and to accompany them on hunting expeditions. He received religious instruction from the chaplain, and training in arms from the 'squires'; he was taught by the ladies of the household to honour and protect all women, and, most importantly, he learned to ride. At 14 he became a squire, when he learned the finer arts of, sword, shield and lance. At 21 he could be made a knight, but only if he had achieved sufficiently high standards in learning and in his household service.

A knight's ideals were to protect the Church, to fight against treachery, to reverence the priesthood, to protect the poor from injustice, to make and keep peace in his own province, to shed blood or, if need be, lay down his life for the sake of the people he had the honour to serve. Whether all knights lived up to these noble aims is another matter!

This was the so-called golden 'age of chivalry', which came to an end with the invention of gunpowder and cannon. However, its principles, its high ideals, were deeply religious and were based on the teachings of Jesus, particularly on his saying: 'For the Son of Man came not to be served but to serve, and to give his life a ransom for many' (Mk. 10.45).

The Christian life involves being, 'in service', that is, in the service of God and our brothers and sisters in Christ. And, it is a service that is not merely a duty, but also an honour and privilege. So let us pray that we might commit ourselves to being 'in service', that we might willingly serve God and our neighbours, for Christ's sake.

> *Lord of peace, as instruments of your love,*
> *may we heal divisions and bring peace.*
> *Forgiving Lord, as we have been forgiven,*
> *help us to forgive others and ourselves.*
> *Serving Lord, who served the Father's will,*
> *help us to serve you with joy,*
> *and willingly continue in your service, all*
> *our days.*
> *Amen.*

In silence

When I was a university chaplain, I took a group of students away for a weekend retreat. Some of the students had never been on a retreat before and some of them found the periods of silence difficult to deal with.

The plan of the retreat was quite simple. There were short sessions during which I would guide their thoughts along the theme they had asked me to explore, after which there would be a longer period spent in silence.

The students were free to walk in the open air, or go to a chapel, or a library or to their rooms. They could pray, read or simply 'be still' in the presence of God, thinking and meditating on the theme. What they could not do was talk. The retreat ended with a service of Holy Communion, and then we all went home.

When we next met up on the campus, I was surprised to learn of the effect on the students of those relatively few periods of silence on the retreat. They told me that they had found the experience 'shattering; mind-blowing'. Several people came to me to discuss the possibility of a change of direction in their way of life. Three people wondered if they should offer for ordination training.

Being still and silent, in the presence of God can open up our minds to all kinds of possibilities that we have never considered before. Most of us are rarely silent. Even in prayer we talk continuously; in our minds, we struggle to put our thoughts into words. We rarely come in silence before God, saying nothing, asking nothing, simply being still in God's presence. Sometimes we make it very difficult for God actually to get a word in edgeways.

Perhaps when we next have a moment to pray, we might try being silent, simply being still in the presence of God, just for a few minutes. At the very least, we will have 'rested in the Lord', which will do us a lot of good.

> *Dear Lord and Father . . .*
> *Drop thy still dews of quietness*
> *Till all our strivings cease:*
> *Take from our souls the strain and stress,*
> *And let our ordered lives confess*
> *The beauty of thy peace.*
>
> *Breathe through the heats of our desire*
> *Thy coolness and thy balm;*
> *Let sense be dumb, let flesh retire;*
> *Speak through the earthquake, wind and*
>   *fire,*
> *O still, small voice of calm.*
> *Amen.*
>   *John Greenleaf Whittier (1807–92)*

In the stars

Some years ago, I interviewed the late Dr Magnus Pyke who was, at the time, a very well-known scientist and television broadcaster. He was famous for the extraordinary gyrations his hands and arms went through when he explained some scientific theory. It was almost as if his limbs were being manipulated by a puppeteer who hadn't quite got the hang of it yet.

I began by asking, 'Magnus, what are your objections to astrology and fortune telling?' Both of his hands flew through a variety of arcs and circles before coming to rest on either side of his face.

'My main objection is – that it isn't true. It's false.' He crossed and uncrossed his legs, twice. 'How can a hack, working for a tabloid newspaper, know whether it is a good day for me to take part in broadcasting, or invest my money, or whatever? It's all rubbish!' His left arm scratched his right ear from behind his head. I thought I'd try another tack.

'Astrologers present arguments suggesting that the heavenly bodies affect the earth and therefore affect us. Is that in any way true?

The arms took flight. 'No evidence! His left hand shot above his head. 'Look, supposing your parents said, "I want you to be a Leo, or a Virgo or whatever." By inducing your birth you can change your star. It's as silly as that.' He began to conduct the *New World* symphony in the air. 'The Mars effect! Somebody had the great idea that if you were born when Mars was in a certain constellation, you'd be a great athlete. And they took out all the Sebastian Coes, all the great athletes and checked their birthdays against the stars and found there was absolutely nothing in it! I am a scientist, I believe in science, I do not believe in what these credulous people, reading the back page of the *Daily Whatever* believe.'

'Would you say you believed in God?'

'It depends on what you mean by God.' (How did I know he was going to say that?) 'Here' – an arm indicated where – 'we have this marvellous system, the universe.' The arms could not resist describing 'the universe'. 'I do believe in a God who has created this extraordinary and wonderful system, and yes, presumably it is something I believe in by faith, to that extent, I do. But!' his right hand gave an imaginary log a karate chop, 'I don't believe in somebody with a long beard who is going to change the laws of science.'

'So you do believe in a creator?'

'Yes, in a kind of misty way, because this total cosmos, the universe, is so strange. You see – *light* – travels at certain speeds, as you are well aware, as we are whizzing round the sun. As you go towards light, you would expect to go faster – and slower as you went away from it, wouldn't you?'

I nodded. 'But scientists have discovered that it is a cock-eyed universe, and whether you are going towards it or going away from it, the speed of light is *exactly* the same! It's like a sock pulled out of shape

106

– that's what the universe is. And I feel a great reverence when these things are brought to our attention
– by scientists.' Both arms point to the heavens. I look
up, and for the first time I become aware that angels
– archangels, cherubim and seraphim – are all wearing white coats, looking into microscopes and singing
Pythagoras' theorem in four-part harmony.

> *O source of all knowledge, life and*
> *   thought,*
> *forgive the childlike foolishness*
> *of faith in signs and omens,*
> *and the absurdity of claiming*
> *that only that which is observable by*
> *   science*
> *has any meaning.*
> *As we attempt to measure the height and*
> *   depth*
> *of the created order, which is your being,*
> *remind us once more of your ineffable*
> *   nature:*
> > *'Thou art a sea without a shore,*
> > *A sun without a sphere;*
> > *Thy time is now and evermore,*
> > *Thy place is everywhere.'*
> *In spite of our cynicism and short-*
> *   sightedness,*
> *enable us to appreciate the gift of Jesus*
> *   Christ,*
> *who, through his loving and Holy Spirit,*
> *bridges your eternity and our now. Amen.*

Inspiration

Martin Luther said that he wrote best when he was angry: anger accelerated his thinking. Charles Dickens did not have to invent stories; he said, they were shown to him by some beneficent power and all he did was write down what he saw. Rudyard Kipling talked about his 'daemon', or muse, that seemed almost to guide his pen.

Many writers talk about the act of writing, the actual putting of pen to paper as a creative process in itself. I have a motto glued to the side of my word processor, which reads: 'The trick is to start writing' and it is true that once you start to move the pen across the page, or your fingers across the keyboard, something magical seems to happen, as one word, one idea leads to another.

Writers of integrity believe that their work is about exploring, discovering and defining truth, but in the end it can only be truth as the writer perceives it. In situations of conflict one group might be called 'terrorists' but, if you believe in their cause, you might call them 'freedom-fighters'.

As children, at the cinema we watched westerns in which the 'goodies' and 'baddies' were clearly defined. The US Cavalry were the 'goodies' and the 'Red Indians' were the 'baddies'. In reality, it was the 'Indians' who were oppressed, and the American army which did much of the oppressing.

It is said that if you really want to know the truth about a particular period of history, you should turn not to the historians, but to the storytellers, the playwrights and the poets, because they capture the feeling, the essence, of what it was like to live at a particular time, or to have known a particular man or woman. Charles Dickens did write down what he saw. As a journalist he had first-hand experience of the richness and the poverty, the generosity and the meanness of the Victorian age, and he described it with extraordinary skill.

True religion is not about historical events, or even theological argument; it is about those personal experiences which, in our struggle to understand, we can only describe as 'spiritual'. It is about an experience of a kind of love that demands a response, that proclaims generosity, pity, forgiveness, kindness and humility as virtues that give depth to our lives. It is the recognition that, ultimately, love is the only thing that makes sense or gives any real meaning to our lives, and that perhaps the highest moment of inspiration experienced by any human being was the moment when a few thousand years ago, a particular writer, struggling to understand the meaning of his own existence, wrote the following three words in this particular order: God is love.

> *Lord,*
> *inspire our thoughts*
> *and colour our words*
> *with your love.*
>
> *Make our lives bright with laughter,*
> *our speech gentle,*

our thinking warm,
our actions kind.

May all we suffer or enjoy
in the spectrum of our days
mellow and blend
in peace and love and praise.
Amen.

Joy

In the American Declaration of Independence, Thomas Jefferson included 'the pursuit of happiness' among those things that he believed to be the 'inalienable right' of all human beings. However, I can't help but wonder if the word 'joy' might have been preferable to 'happiness'. I think 'joy' is a state of being, something that makes us what we are, whereas 'happiness' is something we experience from time to time.

I don't think anyone is likely to live 'happily ever after'. Hopefully most of us will have moments of happiness, times we can look back on and say, 'Yes, that was a happy time', but unless we live under exceptional circumstances we all, from time to time, have to do work which we would rather not do, and deal with situations we find unsatisfactory or difficult. In these moments it is unlikely that we will be happy – and yet, I believe it is possible to go through a difficult time, and still hold on to a deep-rooted joy. For example, the knowledge of love is a source of joy. The fact that I know I am loved by my wife or children is a joy I can possess even if I am in pain.

When Jesus was teaching his disciples about loving one another as he had loved them, he said, 'I have said these things to you so that my joy may be in you, and that your joy may be complete' (Jn. 15.11). He said these things on the night in which he knew Judas was about to betray him. He was not talking about happiness, but about an assurance of the knowledge of the love of God that would sustain him and remain with him, no matter what happened. This is the joy that Jesus wants us to have.

It might be a strange thing to say, but it is sometimes in grief that people realize, or discover for the first time, the real depth of the love of God, and the love of others. In grief they find they are sustained by a depth of love they didn't know existed. Sometimes in grief we are surprised by joy.

It is not that we need to be people of massive grit, determination and character, it is simply a matter of accepting that we are loved by God and by those he has given us to love. And then, as St Paul said, with that love deep down inside, we can face anything in creation, in life and in death, with the joy of knowing that that love will never leave us.

> *Lord of life and love,*
> *if true joy lies in the perception*
> *of the eternal love which surrounds us,*
> *may there be, this day, at least one*
>   *moment*
> *when we perceive your presence in our*
>   *midst.*
> *Amen.*

Labels and pigeon-holes

I was once involved in a party game where a cardboard headband was put on each person, on which were written certain words. The person wearing the headband, though, did not know what the words were.

We sat in a circle and were given a subject to discuss as normally as possible, but with the instruction to treat each person according to the words written on their headband. Looking around the group I could see headbands which said: 'I am very, very young – be patient with me'; 'I am very old – speak slowly'; 'I am a very insignificant person – ignore me'; 'I am deaf – speak clearly and loudly'.

The idea was to work out what your label was by the way in which people spoke to you. It also revealed the prejudices we have about people when we keep them pigeon-holed according to their age, sex, health, status or nationality. For example, there is a tendency to assume that if someone is very old, they have automatically lost their powers of intelligent conversation.

I remember a highly articulate and extremely well-read old man telling me that he and his wife had a home help who always spoke to them as if they were senile. He said that by the time she left each day, both he and his wife were behaving in a senile manner. She would say, no doubt in what she thought to be a very kindly way, 'Hello. And how are we today?' nodding her head with such vigorous encouragement that it was difficult for them not to start nodding back as if they had lost the use of their brains, and answering in the senile way she expected.

Labelling people reduces them to the size of the label, and the sad thing is that we are all inclined to do it. It happens very easily: people do something wrong, perhaps just once, but they are labelled with that mistake, or misunderstanding, for the rest of their lives.

It is a bad habit that we can all slip into. I often find that people I have slotted into a mental pigeon-hole are revealed as altogether different. Someone says, 'Do you know the Reverend XYZ?' Immediately an image flashes into my mind of the Reverend XYZ making what I thought to be a rather silly remark at a meeting, 'Oh yes, I remember him.' Then the other person says, 'Wonderful man. When Richard died I don't know how I would have survived if it hadn't been for his thoughtfulness and kindness.' And once again I am chastened to realize that people are far richer and more complex than my mental labelling and pigeon-holing allows.

Imagine if God were to label us permanently by our sins; we would never lift our heads again. But God is more merciful than we are: in God's sight we are all equal, regardless of age, sex, nationality, culture or reputation. And thank God for that.

Holy Spirit, Father and Mother of us all,
as in your sight we are remembered not for

our sins, but as children in need of love and reconciliation, give us, we pray, the same generosity of spirit that will enable us to see all those we encounter as sisters and brothers. We ask it in and through our Lord and Saviour Jesus Christ, in whose name we are recognized as sons and daughters of God.
Amen.

Lancelot Andrewes, an 'honest-to-God' man

In 1555, nine years before the birth of Shakespeare, Lancelot Andrewes, the son of a sea captain, was born in Barking in Essex. He was an exceptionally bright and clever boy, especially good at languages, and he was given special educational advantages. He spent 15 years at Pembroke College, Cambridge, first as a student, then as a Fellow. Later he became Master of Pembroke College.

Andrewes became the Dean of Westminster, and then Bishop of Ely, Bishop of Chichester and Bishop of Winchester. He was a Privy Counsellor to King James I, he was involved in translating the King James Version of the Bible, and he preached the funeral sermon of Queen Elizabeth I. It was in preaching that he really came into his own, and for which he is best remembered. He had a wonderful 'prayer before preaching': 'O God, I open my mouth wide. Do thou fill it.'

In the eyes of the world Lancelot Andrewes must have seemed an exceptionally successful man but he saw himself in a very different light. In fact, it was only after his death, when people came across his battered, stained and clearly much-used book of 'Private Prayers', that people began to realize his real depth.

The book was obviously never intended to be read by anyone but himself. It was written untidily, in no particular order. Sometime a page would contain just a single sentence, sometimes there were just scribbled notes, phrases or headings. In addition he didn't write in English; so much did he want to keep these thoughts private that all his jottings were either in Hebrew or Greek. This was the place where he poured out his innermost, deepest and most personal thoughts.

He berated himself for not having enough compassion for the poor, and because he had not ministered sufficiently to their needs. He castigated himself for evil thoughts, for unkind words to his colleagues and friends. Here was a man famous for his scholarship, his preaching, his translations of the Bible, and yet in his private prayers he wrote: 'I have not studied to seek and know thee as I ought. Knowing thee, I have not glorified thee, nor given thanks accordingly. I have drawn near to thee with my lips, but my heart has been far from thee.'

Whatever rewards the world heaped on Lancelot Andrewes, he was a man who walked humbly before God, and never lost sight of his true humanity. His 'Private Prayers' reveal that, in a world of high politics and glittering prizes, he was a humble man and, above all else, 'honest to God'. Considering the story of his life, perhaps that was his highest achievement.

> *Give us, O Lord, the humility*
> *to acknowledge our ignorance and to seek*
> *   your wisdom;*
> *and the honesty to know our weakness*
> *   and to seek your strength;*
> *for Jesus Christ's sake.*
> *Amen.*

Life is . . .

When I first worked for BBC local radio, I was employed as a general producer. I was responsible for a wide range of programmes. I produced a music magazine, I was the farming producer, the religious programmes' producer, the short-story editor, I presented a comedy record programme on Saturday mornings, and I was also the weekend continuity announcer. With so many programmes to fill every week, it was hard going sometimes to find sufficient material to produce them all.

One ploy was to go out with a tape recorder, find five or six reasonably well-known people: actors or comedians at the local touring theatre, politicians or local dignitaries, and ask them an impossible question like: 'If you were God for an hour, what would you change?' or 'If you could be somebody else who would you be?' Then you turned their answers into a feature. Having done this sort of thing once or twice you recognize the ploy when you see it; it happens on 'thin' news days, when there is a lot of space to fill.

I saw an example of it in a national newspaper once, when the big question was 'What is the meaning of life?' The answers included one from an eminent professor who said, 'Just because you can ask a question, it does not follow that there has to be an answer.' (Thank you, Professor.) The boxer, Chris Eubank said: 'The meaning of life is to do good.' And Alexei Sayle, the comedian, said: 'I don't know the meaning of life, but I do know the meaning of "Eichhörnchen" – it's German for squirrel.'

That 'big question' filler set me off looking for other definitions. Alan Bennett's vicar, in the revue *Beyond the Fringe*, said: 'Life – is rather like a tin of sardines – we are all looking for the key.' And American writer and humorist Fran Lebowitz once said: 'Life – is something to do when you can't get to sleep.' There is also a wonderful 'Life is . . . ' quote in the Talmud, which says: 'We might want life to be like the shadow of a tree cast against a wall – but actually, life is like the shadow of a bird in flight.'

Of course, *any* attempt to define the meaning of life is doomed to failure since life is 'a bowl of cherries' and at the same time it is also 'a vale of tears'. It's about doing good, loving and laughing; and it's about grief and pain and regret. But here is *my* 'Life is . . .' statement that I hope might give you pause for thought: 'Life is a series of discoveries – which raise more questions than we have time to answer; making "eternal life" at the very least, a possibility.'

> *Loving God, in whose being lies the path to understanding all things, and who through your Son Jesus Christ guides us in our search for meaning and truth, help us always to keep open minds, loving hearts and the ability to celebrate the fact of life itself. Amen.*

Life plan

The other day I received an advertising fax that said in very large letters: 'It's never too late to consider a new 'life plan'. 'Oh yes it is,' I said, screwing up the fax paper and getting a 'hole in one' in the waste-paper basket. A 'life plan'? I wish I had one, and I don't mean an insurance policy.

I did a one-man show at Leeds University once, for a national conference of prison chaplains. After the show, a prison governor said to me, 'I made a note of something you said tonight. You said, "You don't plan your life, do you? It just kind of 'happens' to you." Well,' he added, 'I can tell you, nobody leaves school saying – "I want to work in the Prison Service" – nobody! But somehow, they find they are in it.' It's strange how life does just sort of 'happen' to you.

I think a lot of us start out saying, 'I'd like to be a nurse, a farmer, a teacher', or whatever, but most of us end up doing something else entirely. And whatever we do for a living, many of us harbour secret dreams of doing something else.

Dreams are fine, providing we can cope with the quirkiness of reality as well; such as the fact that one day we turn left instead of right, fall in love, make mistakes or find a curious satisfaction in an unex-pected area, and we are drawn into a way of life that we could never have 'planned', even in our wildest dreams.

Of course, there are some single-minded, one-track individuals who say, 'That is what I want, and that is where I'm going.' The trouble with such single-minded ambition is that the goal keeps moving. It is always just out of reach. Life will be wonderful when . . . I've done that . . . got this . . . achieved the other. It makes it very difficult to enjoy the present moment, to be happy now.

Personally, I think we can all have successful 'bits' of life, which might have nothing to do with work or careers. Most of us have moments when we love what we are doing, and the people we are doing it with; so, when the grandchildren visit, enjoy the moments; when you have coffee with a good friend, enjoy that moment too. That's a good 'life plan': live now, not later or, as Jesus said, 'Don't be anxious for tomorrow, tomorrow will be anxious for itself.'

> *Eternal God, give us the wisdom neither to dwell in the past nor to be a prisoner of tomorrow's dreams, but grant us the gift of being able to live in and enjoy the present moment; the place where you are, the eternal now.*
> *Amen.*

Like a child

Every now and then, the BBC reruns the comedy series *The Good Life*. If I happen to be flicking through the channels and catch sight of Margo Leadbetter laying down the law to a local council employee, I'm hooked.

On the bookshelves in our house are a number of volumes on the subject of self-sufficiency. They recall the days when my wife and I had a smallholding and were deeply immersed in the then growing popularity of the idea of being self-supporting in growing food, and as self-sufficient in every other area as possible. At that time *The Good Life*, with Richard Briers and Felicity Kendal as a couple trying to become self-sufficient in suburbia, was one of the most popular series on television. So on our shelves are books about rearing sheep and pigs, about farmers or beef cattle, crops, land management, vets, fencing and field drainage. At a time when many people were talking about the possibility of the breakdown of society, as the world's natural resources diminished, self-sufficiency began to sound very attractive.

The idea was to become as self-sufficient as possible so that you needed little help from anyone else to obtain your daily bread. On the other hand, the richness of life is to do with our relationships with other people, with involvement with our neighbours, interchange, sharing a common goal, making a life together.

One of the reasons why *The Good Life* was so popular was that it was really about the day-to-day life of neighbours. It is interesting to reflect that neither the Goods nor the Leadbetters had any children, although you could say that the Leadbetters were the 'grown-ups' and the Goods were the 'children'. Children and babies, of course, are exactly the opposite of self-sufficient. They are totally dependent on others for everything.

Children do not earn either their food or their clothing; they simply accept what it is given to them. As we grow older we seem to find it more difficult to accept gifts or even help. People are sometimes offended by gifts: 'I don't need charity. I have my pride, you know' is the phrase you sometimes hear.

Actually, we *do* need charity, both in giving and receiving. To understand and to receive the grace of God, we need, as Jesus said, 'to become like little children' who are not self-sufficient, not independent, and not too proud to accept help, gifts, love and forgiveness.

It is a process of learning that does not end with childhood. Pride makes demands, creates rules and stands on its dignity whilst the humility of 'childlikeness' has a simplicity that sits lightly to 'rules' and can laugh at itself. I suppose when we begin to understand the joy of true simplicity, we have really begun to live the 'good' life.

This prayer was written by Johann Starck in the eighteenth century for his child. He is praying for the whole life of his child but also I think he is praying

that the child will never lose the simplicity and humility of a child, even in old age.

> *Lord, my God, let the light of your love*
>   *fall on my child.*
> *Keep him safe from illness and injury.*
> *Enter his infant soul, and comfort him*
>   *with your peace and joy.*
> *Being too young to speak, his cries and*
>   *gurgles have no meaning for me.*
> *But to your ears they are prayers.*
> *His cries are cries for your blessing.*
> *His gurgles are delight at your grace.*
> *As a child, may he learn your ways.*
> *As a man, let him live the full span of life,*
>   *serving your kingdom on earth.*
> *And finally in his old age,*
> *let him die in sure and certain knowledge*
>   *of your salvation.*
> *I do not ask that he may have wealth,*
>   *power or fame.*
> *But I ask that he may have simplicity of*
>   *spirit,*
> *humility in his vocation, and devotion in*
>   *worship.*
> *Dear Lord, smile on him.*
> *Amen.*
>
>   *Johann Starck (1680–1756)*

Living in faith

In 1522, Martin Luther in the introduction to his commentary on St Paul's letter to the Romans, wrote: 'This letter is the *principal* part of the New Testament – and the purest Gospel.' According to Martin Luther not only should we know it by heart, but we should consider its meaning for our lives – every day.

Paul's letter to the Romans opened up the meaning of the Christian faith for Martin Luther. This was the letter that released him, that enabled him to see that we are not saved by good works, we don't earn salvation by prayers or by charitable acts, but we are saved by faith through grace and the love of God. We are required to live the life of faith. So how do we live such a life?

Faith is not merely believing in certain ideas, or simply accepting doctrinal statements. Faith is also about relationship. 'Living in faith' means trusting someone, or being at one with someone. I can give you a very good example of what it means to trust someone.

Years ago, when I was performing songs with Donald Swann in a theatre in London, every night was a completely different performance – we sang the same songs but never in exactly the same way. Donald Swann was a genius at playing the piano. He could, of course, have played from a musical score, but instead he had a copy of the lyrics with a few scribbled notes in the margins such as key signatures B flat or F sharp. That was all he needed, the rest was in his head. But he never, ever played the same accompaniment twice, and I was never sure what was going to come out.

Sometimes he would launch off into a flight of musical fantasy and I just had to trust that if I stuck to my part, even though I didn't know where he was going, we would somehow reach the end of the song at exactly the same moment as each other – and we always did. I came to realize that he would never let me down, I just had to trust him. Now that, I suppose, is an example of one kind of 'living in faith'. Christian 'living in faith' is about living in a relationship of absolute trust, with Jesus Christ.

> *Almighty God,*
> *who calls us to venture along paths we*
>   *have never trod;*
> *where the end cannot always be seen,*
> *plant within us confidence in your*
>   *unfailing love*
> *that, putting all our trust in you, we might*
>   *truly live in faith.*
> *Amen.*

Love is the greatest thing

If ever there was an over-used, misused, misunderstood word, that word must be love. 'I *love* Greek yoghurt and honey' in reality means 'I greatly enjoy Greek yoghurt and honey.' 'I *loved* Pavorotti' means 'I enjoyed his singing.'

Love is far more than merely *liking*. People have been known to do costly, sacrificial things for love of their fellow human beings, even those who were not very lovable. I remember a colleague, a minister, who was trying to help some very difficult and awkward people, saying to me, 'I keep having to remind myself that although it is my calling to *love* these blessed people, I don't necessarily have to *like* them.'

But then consider the love demonstrated in the life of Jesus Christ, and his teaching: 'Greater love has no one than they lay down their lives for love of their friends . . . Anyone can love their friends, but I tell you to love your enemies.' Jesus died loving those who persecuted him and asking for forgiveness for those who reviled him.

Throughout history there have been many dramatic stories of people who have laid down their lives for others, people like Dietrich Bonhoeffer who prayed for his executioners when he was put to death at the end of the Second World War. There are, of course, less dramatic stories of people who have sacrificed their lives for love over many years, those who have nursed disabled or perhaps terminally ill people, who have given their lives not in one dramatic act, but by sacrificing perhaps their prime years for the sake of someone else. On the other hand, the truly loving person does not think in terms of sacrifice or reward. Love is, in itself, its own reward.

Possibly the best description of the nature of love is to be found in the letter that Paul wrote to the Corinthians:

> Love is patient; love is kind;
> love is not envious or boastful or
> arrogant or rude.
> It does not insist on its own way,
> it is not irritable or resentful;
> it does not rejoice in wrongdoing but rejoices
> in the truth.
> It bears all things,
> believes all things,
> hopes all things,
> endures all things.
> Love never ends . . .
> And now faith, hope and love abide, these
> three,
> and the greatest of these is love.

1 Cor. 13.4–8, 13

Almighty God, in the loves of our lives
give us generous, loving hearts,
that we might, like your shadow,
imitate the perfect love you have shown us
in and through Jesus Christ, our Lord.
Amen.

Love story

I went to an end-of-term Speech Day at a school where, a few years earlier, I had been a teacher and the school chaplain. It is a salutary experience, trying to recognize children who, in the space of a few years, have been magically transformed into young adults. One young woman reminded me of a class in which we had played a storytelling game. It had been the end of term, exams had been done and reports written, and we were having fun.

The game consisted of one team giving subjects or objects to be included in a story to be made up by another team. At first, the subjects included heart-throbs like Mel Gibson and Tom Cruise, mainly stories about romantic entanglements. The game had been going for some time when one team, trying, I suspect, to be provocative, asked their opponents to tell a story that was about robbers, violence and love, in which all the characters were men.

After they had finished their whispered huddle the storytellers began to tell their story. I wondered how they were going to deal with it. They had not got far when, suddenly, I recognized the story. I was delighted by their ingenuity. They attempted to disguise the characters, to dress them up in modern clothes, to set the action in an American city and to cast some famous film stars in the principle parts, but it became quite clear to me that they were telling the story of the Good Samaritan. This was the story that Jesus told about a man set upon by robbers, left for dead and rescued by a traveller who belonged to an outcast community. The storytellers had fulfilled all the criteria: it *is* a story about robbers and violence, and all the characters are men, but it is also about the selfless loving actions of one man towards a total stranger.

I asked the young woman I had taught if she remembered that story being told. 'Oh yes,' she said. 'I'm a freelance writer now, and I actually wrote a version of that story for a magazine, only this time all the characters were women. After all, you told us that it was about the love of God, so it's not a story about sex, it's about generosity and sacrifice.'

I suppose our meeting was a case of 'the teacher being taught'!

> *Lord, let me reflect the colours of your*
>   *love.*
> *Let my life be bright with laughter,*
> *my speech gentle, my thinking warm, my*
>   *actions kind.*
> *May all I suffer or enjoy, in the spectrum*
>   *of my days,*
> *mellow and blend, in peace, in love, in*
>   *praise.*
> *Amen.*

Loving your enemy

Every year, the Churches Advertising Network in the UK produces a special poster for Easter, the object of which is to make people stop and think. Some posters are more successful than others; people are completely unmoved, or puzzled or even outraged by them. Once the poster consisted of an image of the head of Christ crowned with thorns, and it looked remarkably like a well-known image of Che Guevara, the South American revolutionary leader.

The picture was *meant* to be controversial and to raise questions about the person of Jesus Christ. Using the face of an internationally famous revolutionary as the face of Christ questioned the popular image of Jesus as 'gentle Jesus, meek and mild'.

In his own time, far from being seen as 'meek and mild', he was perceived by many of his contemporaries as a threat to established religion and to the state. One of the reasons for his execution was the fear that he might have led an uprising against the occupying forces of the Roman Empire. A previous uprising had been put down earlier with such barbaric cruelty by the Romans that it was not surprising that a number of Jewish leaders were very edgy about at the possibility of another. And it is a fact that Jesus *did* challenge traditional religious ceremonies and rites – he questioned the integrity of the religious laws about almsgiving, and he even criticized the manner in which people prayed.

In many ways his teachings *were* revolutionary, but they were far from encouraging anyone to rise up against the Romans. Look at these verses from Matthew's Gospel:

> 'You have heard that it was said: "You shall love your neighbour and hate your enemy." But I say to you, Love your enemies and pray for those who persecute them . . . if anyone strikes you on the right cheek, turn the other also; and if anyone wants to sue you and take your coat, give your cloak as well; and if anyone forces you to go one mile, go also the second mile.'
>
> Matt. 5.38–41

Now *that* was revolutionary!

Jesus, teacher and redeemer,
who turns upside down all our concepts
of kingdoms, power and authority,
create a revolution in my heart,
and in the hearts of all who love you,
that we might embrace your revolutionary
   love
in which the first is last and the last first
and the highest rank in your kingdom is
   servant.
Amen.

Making things happen

I was once in a church hall signing copies of my auto-biography and afterwards I got into conversation with two women, one of whom had read my book. She said, 'You seem to have done so many things. Why is it, do you think, that some people have all sorts of adventures, compared to others who do not?'

I replied, 'Well, I hope this doesn't sound too trite, but I believe that nothing happens until you do something. It is no good sitting at home waiting for adventure to happen, you have to stimulate it. It almost doesn't matter what you do: join a drama society, a club, a writers' circle, a ramblers' associa-tion, go on a mystery bus ride: but get involved, and one thing leads to another. As the Bible says, "Cast your bread upon the waters and it will come back to you an hundredfold."'

At this point the other lady, who had been quietly listening to all this, said, 'Oh, I couldn't agree more. I cast my bread on the water when I was feeling at my lowest and it has come back not just a hundredfold but three, four or five hundredfold.'

And she told a fascinating story about how, after the death of her husband, she had struggled to come to terms with the disabling numbness of grief. She and her husband had been so close that when he died, she felt that the whole point and purpose of her life had died with him. In time, however, she realized that her life would go on – the world would continue to turn and she needed to make a new life for herself.

She wasn't sure where to start but, on an impulse, she went into a charity shop in her local shopping centre and asked if they could use a volunteer. They welcomed her with open arms. They were raising money for people and countries in crisis in various parts of the world where, year after year, there had been continuous crop failures, earthquakes or wars, where revolution or military coups had left thousands of people displaced and homeless.

At first, the woman helped to sort out the stock at the back of the shop, then later she helped to sell things in the shop. Then the charity needed a part-time paid district organizer based in a nearby town. She went for that job and got it. The part-time job eventually became a full-time job. She then moved on to be a full-time county organizer. The next step was to take a post at national level. After that, she travelled all over the world, visiting projects set up by the charity. She made new friends up and down the country and all over the world. But it all started, she said, because she offered to help in a local charity shop.

She did not say she had offered her life to be used by God, but I suspect that somewhere along the way, consciously or unconsciously, her words, thoughts and actions were translated by the Holy Spirit into a prayer which said, 'Lord, if you can use me in any way, then here I am, use me.' When we make our-selves available to the work of the Holy Spirit there is no telling where that may lead.

Making things happen

*Help us, O God, to live in such a way
that our hearts and minds may be open
to the adventurous guidance of your Holy
   Spirit.
Give us the courage to offer ourselves,
our talents and our time
in the service of Jesus Christ our Lord.
Amen.*

Moments of truth

Some people say that there is no such thing as a *new* idea – but only the discovery, or rediscovery, of a truth that has been with us all the time. Well, old or new, ideas can be both exciting *and* frightening. Exciting, because they can open up new horizons, new possibilities; and frightening, because they can change our whole way of life or reach even deeper and change us as people. I think that 'Damascus road' experiences are more common than we imagine, and that people's lives continue to be changed by moments of insight.

I know a successful photographer, who took up his profession because of something he heard on the radio. His life was in turmoil. He was so caught up in running his business, in surviving, that his days were reduced to two things: work and sleep. Then one day he heard a broadcaster describing exactly his condition, and suggesting that he should take time, make time, to be still, to take a few deep breaths and in calmness and quiet ask himself what things in his life were really important and what were not. So he did exactly what the broadcaster suggested.

He got into his car, drove into the country, stopped in a lay-by and took a few deep breaths. As he sat there he began to see the landscape in front of him. It was a familiar landscape, but it was as if he saw it for the first time, and he was suddenly overcome by the beauty of the natural world. This moment of reflection changed his life. He sold his business and became a photographer.

I once met a film actor, Keiron Moore, who gave up a successful career to work for a charity. He had been filming on location in a poor country, and he was suddenly struck by the huge difference between the lifestyle of the indigenous people and that of the film crew. That moment changed his whole life.

Ideas are dangerous. They can be seen as a threat to some people. The South American Bishop Dom Helder Camara was famous for saying, 'When I feed the poor they call me a saint. When I ask, "Why are the poor hungry?" they call me a communist.' People who have asked such simple and direct questions have often been martyred – killed by those who see such questions as a threat to their way of life. But you cannot murder the truth. Truth has a strange way of coming alive again no matter how many times people attempt to bury it.

In Dennis Potter's wonderful play, *Son of Man*, which is about the Passion and death of Jesus Christ, Pontius Pilate says that ideas are far more dangerous than idealists. It's quite simple really: you can kill the idealist, but an entire army cannot stop the advance of an idea, or a dream. So hold on to your dreams; don't ignore your moments of insight. It is very tempting to push them to the back of your mind because you are afraid of the consequences of acting on them. Frightening though they may be, they are meant to change your life.

Loving God,
comfort us as we attempt to journey in
  your name.
May the light of your love truly enlighten
  our minds
and cast new light on the way we should
  live.
In your mercy, make clear our path
from this day forward and for evermore,
through our Lord and Saviour, Jesus
  Christ.
Amen.

Most loving – most right

There are times when we are presented with dilemmas that make it difficult to know for certain what is the right thing to say or do. I have heard of people who like to refer to someone else whom they know and respect, as a kind of 'rule of thumb'; when faced with a difficult decision they say to themselves, 'Now, what would Abraham Lincoln have done in this situation?' or, more likely, 'What would my mother have said?'

A 'rule of thumb' should be a flexible rule. Trying to live by rigid and inflexible rules is a sure recipe for a great deal of unhappiness. I have my own 'rule of thumb', which some people might find helpful: it is, when in doubt, usually the most loving thing to do is the right thing to do. 'The most loving thing' is not an easy way out. It is not a 'soft' option. Sometimes 'the most loving thing to do' might mean saying 'no' to a child, or it might mean we have to make a considerable personal sacrifice.

A colleague from another church came to me, very troubled about a young person with a severe learning difficulty, who had asked to be baptized.

'What's the problem ?' I asked.

'Well, the first problem is that he has to fill in a form and sign a statement that he understands and accepts the basic tenets of the Christian faith. But he can neither read nor write and I don't think he understands very much about the Christian faith at all. Physically he is an adult, intellectually he is on a par with a four-year-old.'

'What was his actual request?' I said.

'He just said, "I want to be baptized because I love Jesus." '

'That sounds good enough to me,' I said.

'But he has to give intellectual assent. And if he can't fill in the form, how can he do that?'

So I told him about my 'rule of thumb'. 'In this situation,' I said, 'I think that the most loving thing to do is to ignore the form and baptize him.'

'Oh, I can't do that, because the form has to go into a central register.'

'Well, fill it in for him.'

'I couldn't do that, that would be dishonest.'

'Then don't fill in the form, don't send any details to the central register, but just go ahead and baptize him anyway.' He looked genuinely shocked. Then I had a bright idea. I said, 'What do you think Jesus would have done in this case? Do you think he would turn away a child who says, "I love Jesus" '? That seemed to do the trick.

A few weeks later, there was a very happy baptism service, which I was glad to attend. I never did learn what happened about the form, and I was far too discreet to ask.

Most loving – most right

Lord, in all the decisions we have to make,
help us to decide,
not by the letter of the law
but by the spirit of love.
For Jesus Christ's sake.
Amen.

Moving on

Henri Nouwen was a Dutch Catholic priest, who died in 1996. He was a teacher in the Netherlands and in the United States for about 20 years, but he devoted the latter part of his life to working for the L'Arche Daybreak Community in Toronto. The L'Arche communities – there are a number of them in various countries – are like extended family units based in ordinary houses, in which people who have no physical or cerebral problems share their lives with people who do have difficulties of various kinds.

They are communities in which everybody attempts to live as normal a life as possible, according to their abilities. Those who can go out to work, whilst others may be engaged in some form of cottage industry, but each contributes to the community according to their ability. It is an attempt to offer a loving, sharing, ordinary home life to people who might otherwise be institutionalized.

Henri Nouwen, teacher and priest, spent the last years of his life living in one of these communities as a pastor, which meant that he spent a lot of time listening to people who struggled to find meaning and purpose in their lives. It doesn't really matter how well educated you are, or how little education you have had; there are a number of very basic experiences that we all share and needs we all have. From time to time we are all disappointed, angry, hurt or frustrated. Listening to people sharing their problems, Henri Nouwen began to see that people coped with their crises in different ways.

In one of his books, he said that people had to find ways of 'stepping over' their anger, their frustration and their hurt. Some people, he said, circled round and round their bitter experiences. The trouble with going round in circles is that you keep coming back to the same point, you never move on. In fact, some people begin to enjoy circling around their problems and spend years getting nowhere.

The trick, he said, is to look at your anger or frustration, and then, mentally, put it down on the ground, step over it and move on. If you keep circling whatever it is that hurt you, you will be imprisoned by it, but if you step over it and move on, you are a person who has *been* angry, *knows* about hurt and frustration but has not been *overcome* by them, and is richer and stronger because of it.

We all make mistakes. We all make errors of judgement, we all do things we regret. We all need to learn from our mistakes. We all need to pray for those who have offended us, and hope that they too will have learned from their mistakes. We all need to put down on the ground, like heavy stones, the burdens of our errors and misjudgements – and other people's errors and misjudgements – step over them and, without a backward look, move on.

> *Lord, help me to learn from the past,*
> *to live in the present, and to hope for the*
>   *future;*
> *help me to let go of my burdens and move on,*
> *trusting, now and always, in you. Amen.*

Natural praise

One of the great joys of my life at the moment is the appearance of a new generation in our family. It seemed to happen rather quickly. One minute there was just us and the kids, and then the first grandchild arrived; suddenly, there are now eight grandchildren.

One aspect of being a grandparent is that you can watch children develop and grow, and observe them in a way that you couldn't the first time round, perhaps because you were too busy or just too tired.

I'm sure it must be good educational theory that children respond far more positively to praise than they do to criticism. It is marvellous what a little praise will do for a small child; when someone says, 'Oh, that is good! Well done! How clever, how excellent!' the smile spreads, the head lifts and if you measured them I expect you would find that they were a millimetre taller, at least!

It isn't just small children; everybody needs the encouragement of a little praise from time to time. Whether you are a child or a grandparent, everybody needs the acknowledgement of work well done. For example, the basic 'necessities' of life – food and drink – presented to us every day in a variety of forms from a variety of people, are often taken for granted. The work of those who prepared, cooked and gave us our food is accepted with little or no comment, while a simple word of praise or thanks might make a world of difference to that person.

Thanks and praise are stimulants that can change lives. I think that I can say that my whole life, the things I studied, the career I followed, was probably the result of the praise and encouragement I received from a particular teacher at school. In my mind's eye I can still see the classroom and the face of the teacher, whose name was John Farrell. He taught English Language and Literature. He once handed me an essay that he had marked and said, 'This is very good. I think you have a way with words. You could very easily become a writer.'

Years later, when I was working for the BBC, I received some scripts from someone called John Farrell. The name rang a bell, of course, but I never imagined it was my teacher. The scripts were good and I invited him to record them for the programme I was producing. He came to the studio, and he was the same John Farrell, my English teacher. I told him that his praise for my work as a schoolboy had led me to where I now was, writing, editing and producing for the BBC. To complete the story, we enjoyed several co-writing projects in the years that followed. I wonder what might have happened if he had never uttered those words of praise?

What is praise? It isn't flattery, that's false praise. Genuine praise is the natural joyous response to something good that you experience in your life. Of course, that is also what 'praising God' means: responding with joy to the creator and author of all good things.

Loving God, teach us not only to recognize the gifts, graces and talents of those around us but to share that recognition, to give praise where it is due; and in the blessings of each day may we express our thankfulness to you in prayer, with joy and with praise, in the name of Jesus Christ our Lord and Saviour.
Amen.

Neither cold, nor lukewarm

A friend of mine, who was my guide and mentor for many years, and who is still with me in spirit, once said to me, 'You should always welcome people with "bees in their bonnet". You might not be interested in their particular concern, but don't knock them – at the very least they show that they care about something with a certain amount of passion, which is far better than the cynical apathy that turns its back on people's concerns, saying, "It's nothing to do with me, it's not my concern. I don't want to know." You shouldn't be a cold or lukewarm Christian either, the sort of person who agrees "in principle" but is not wholeheartedly committed, the sort of person who says "Somebody should do something about it" but never wants to do anything themselves.' It was advice I have never forgotten.

Thomas More was a man who was 'wholeheartedly committed'. He was a lawyer, politician and author (he wrote the book *Utopia*), a privy councillor and Henry VIII's Lord Chancellor. He fell out of favour with the King because he refused to sign a document accepting Henry as Head of the Church after his divorce from Katherine of Aragon. His friends attempted to persuade him to play along and keep the King happy, saying that it was silly to lose everything over such a small matter of principle. But Thomas was a man of deep commitment and religious belief; he did not play at his Christianity, it meant everything to him. He said that he would rather lose his life than his immortal soul. In the end Henry lost patience with him and signed a warrant for Thomas' execution.

Thomas once wrote a prayer which said: 'My sweet Saviour Christ, who in thine undeserved love towards mankind so kindly wouldst suffer the painful death of the cross, suffer me not to be cold nor lukewarm in love again – towards thee.'

Wholehearted commitment to a cause or a belief certainly intensifies life, and a real Christian faith ought never to be merely lip service. It means utter and total commitment to Jesus. We should all have, as my friend would say, 'a bee in our bonnets' that will not allow us to shut out the truth simply because it is inconvenient to mention it.

Give us, O Lord . . .
a lively faith, a firm hope and fervent love.
Take from us all lukewarmness of spirit
and all dullness in prayer,
and grant that we may labour for that
which we ask of you;
through Jesus Christ our Lord.
Amen.

Thomas More (1478–1535)

Our Father

In the late 1960s, when I was training for the ministry in a Methodist theological college in Bristol, we all had to belong to one of three 'mission bands'. One mission band worked once a week in a local church, another in a hospital, and a third in an 'approved school' for boys who had, for various reasons, come before the courts.

Each year students could move from one 'mission band' to another, except for the one that went to the approved school. If you were in that mission band you stayed in it for three years, because it took a long time to win the confidence of the boys, and to be trusted by them.

A considerable number of these boys had lost the ability to trust anybody. Some felt betrayed, abandoned, unwanted. Most had suffered at the hands of violent parents, or the man who was currently living with their mother, or whoever. Some boys had no idea who their real parents were. To be trusted by them we had to make it very clear that we were not auxiliary or part-time staff, we were simply friends who came ready to listen, talk, play games, help write letters, anything. If we did talk about their experiences, it was under the seal of the confessional, never to be shared with anyone else.

It took time. With some boys it never happened, you never got through the brick wall they had built around their innermost feelings, but sometimes there *was* a breakthrough and a boy would share his hopes and dreams and pain. It did not necessarily mean an ongoing relationship. Having unburdened himself once, he might never speak to you again. When you greeted each other, there might be recognition in his eyes, but he might not want to talk again, ever. But that was all right, because now there was at least one other person who understood something of his experience.

We had to be very careful about how we used the word 'father'. Most of the boys did not trust their fathers, or whoever acted as their 'father'. For some, the word suggested to them anger, fear and violence. There must have been, proportionally, as many bad fathers in the days when Jesus walked the streets of Nazareth and Jerusalem as there are now, and yet Jesus said, 'When you pray, say, Our Father, who art in heaven . . . '.

At the heart of Jesus' mission on earth was the need to reveal the nature of his heavenly Father. It was that which drove his whole being from the earliest days: 'I am about my Father's business.' His Father in heaven was a loving Father who forgave, healed, reconciled and made whole. Jesus taught his followers this through the story of 'the prodigal son', which is sometimes also called the story of 'the waiting father'. In that parable Jesus drew for us a picture of a generous, patient father. This is 'our Father in heaven' who is prepared to forgive his children, no matter what they have done. His children need only turn towards him and he runs out to meet them, to welcome them and celebrate their return. There is no talk of recrimination, only joy because those who were lost have been found. Jesus himself demonstrated in his life all the qualities of his heavenly Father, and said, 'The Father and I are one.' We are called to enter into the same relationship, to enjoy the same extravagant, measureless love.

Whatever our experiences of human fatherhood, through Christ we are enabled to put our trust in God, our Father.

> *Father, we pray for those who find it*
>   *difficult to put their trust in you,*
> *who doubt your love, who cannot pray,*
>   *who have lost their faith,*
> *who find it hard to put their trust in*
>   *anyone;*
> *in your mercy, comfort, heal and restore*
>   *your children to their rightful minds,*
>   *that they may find peace in you, for the*
>   *sake of your Son, Jesus Christ, our Lord,*
>   *friend and brother.*
> *Amen.*

Parable

This is a story about aquatic nymphs. It is a parable, which, like all the best parables, speaks for itself:

Aquatic nymphs, as their name implies, live in water, in fact, somewhat below the surface of the water, in streams, ponds and freshwater pools. This particular group lay comfortably half in and half out of the silt on the bed of a very gently moving stream. They had spent all of their lives in the shadow of the stems of some voluptuous water lilies. It was a rich and beautiful world in which they lived. Plant life of all shapes and sizes swayed in the water and reached up from the muddy bed of the stream. There were also many different kinds of living creatures sharing the stream with them. A considerable variety of fish swam by, as did tadpoles in their hundreds and water beetles in their thousands.

The aquatic nymphs marvelled at it all and thought how privileged they were to live in such a wonderful world. One day they saw one of their fellow nymphs lose hold of the silt and very slowly float up and up until eventually he disappeared. Another struggled to the stem of a water lily and began to climb up and up until eventually he also disappeared, and never came back.

A pattern began to emerge. Day after day, nymph after nymph seemed to lose hold of the silt, float, or crawl up and up, and then disappear, and none of them ever came back. The aquatic nymphs who remained on the bed of the stream decided that they had to find out what happened to the nymphs who had gone away. There were rumours that up above, beyond the light that seemed to gleam above their heads, there was an entirely different world, a kind of paradise so magical that it made the stream bed seem rather dull. However, as no nymph ever returned once they had ascended, 'paradise above' remained nothing more than rumour and wishful thinking.

It was decided that whichever nymph next made the ascent up and away from the bed of the stream, that nymph would observe what there was to see and then, whatever happened, they would return and tell all the other nymphs. They all promised solemnly. Quite soon one of the nymphs felt an irresistible urge to let himself slip free from the silt and began to float up and up. As he approached the great light he remembered his promise to return and tell the others of his great adventure.

He had no memory of breaking the surface of the water, nor could he remember how long he had rested on the lily leaf that floated on the surface. He only knew that some kind of transition had happened. Some kind of change in him. When he tried to move he had a strange feeling of lifting above the water. Then, he had the shock of his life. He *was* above the water!

Looking down he could see his reflection in the slow-moving stream, same eyes, same legs, but not quite the same body. Most extraordinary of all, he had wings! Diaphanous, golden wings! He was filled with an incredible feeling of freedom. He was free of the silt, free of the water and he could fly!

He could not resist sweeping over the surface of the water, and then landing on a gentle waving reed. His eyes attempted to take in all the wonders he could see, the incredible light, the colours, the life around him – this was indeed a paradise. Then, once more, he remembered his promise to return to the nymphs and tell them all he had seen and all that would, in time, happen to them. Again and again he flew down to the surface of the water, but no matter how hard he tried, he could not go back. Finally, somewhat exhausted, he stopped trying and rested on a reed.

A frog, who was sitting on a nearby lily pad, had been watching. He had remained silent until now, when he said, 'I have seen a number of you dragonflies diving at the water as if they wanted to swim below the surface. Can't think why you do it, because you're a dragonfly, and dragonflies fly, they don't swim.' Then he hopped off the lily pad into the long grass and disappeared.

The new dragonfly gently lifted off from the reed and hovered over the water staring once again at his reflection. 'So that's what I am, a dragonfly!' And he set off to explore his wonderful new world. He was a little sad that he had not been able to go back and tell the others, but it did not matter really. In time, they would all follow the same route, and even the most cynical would discover that the rumour of 'paradise' was not a rumour, but fact.

People doubt, question or deny the possibility of life after death. Jesus did not only teach with words, with stories, he taught also with his life. He preached love and lived it. He declared truth and demonstrated it. He promised resurrection and his wounded feet walked to Emmaus and his pierced hands broke bread. His promises about life after death were unequivocal: 'I go to prepare a place for you. If it were not so, I would have told you.'

> *Lord of eternity, endless space and all*
>   *creation,*
> *your being is too great for me to envisage*
>   *and the promise of resurrected life*
>   *beyond my imagining,*
> *but I know that neither love nor truth can*
>   *die,*
> *and you are perfect love and perfect truth.*
> *Lord, I believe. Help my unbelief.*
> *Amen.*

Prayer: a take-away service?

When we turn to God in prayer, it is only human to assume that we know exactly what we need to sort out our problems. Our prayers are frequently a list of requests for God to give us precisely what we ask for. I sometimes wonder if God, as we call him up and put in our orders, doesn't feel like some kind of divine take-away service: 'Dear God, would you please give me this, and also a little of that, and, if it's not too much trouble, a smidgeon of the other – and, by the way, can you deliver within the hour?'

William Shakespeare is not the first person you would automatically turn to for advice on prayer and yet, curiously enough, whenever he does make an observation about God, or prayer, his observations are usually quite profound. In *Antony and Cleopatra*, he wrote: 'We, ignorant of ourselves, beg often our own harms, which the wise powers deny us for our good; so find we profit by losing our prayers.'

In other words, sometimes we are better off when our prayers are not answered, particularly when we ask for the wrong things. In the garden of Gethsemane Jesus gave us a great insight into the heart of prayer when he prayed, 'Father, not my will, but your will be done.' At the inner core of prayer is a relationship, a spiritual relationship with God. Prayer is not simply a recital of religious words and phrases. It is a relationship based on love and trust, and built on a commitment to the will of God. Words alone will not achieve prayer. Shakespeare had something to say about this, too. In *Hamlet*, he says, 'My words fly up, my thoughts remain below: Words without thoughts never to heaven go.'

When we are unwell and visit a doctor, we do not tell our doctor what he or she should give us, we put our trust in their special knowledge and accept their advice. Similarly, prayer is coming before God, confessing our need and putting our trust in God's special knowledge of us, and then accepting the guidance that will be offered through the Holy Spirit.

> *Loving God, physician of our souls, you know us and our needs better than we do ourselves. As your children, we ask that we might stand in the shadow of Jesus, and pray with him, 'Father, not my will, but your will be done.'*
> *Amen.*

Praying for peace

It used to be a kind of running joke that contestants in beauty contests, when asked about their interests always included in their answer 'world peace'. But maybe we shouldn't have laughed; they were only reflecting a worldwide longing for peace. No one in their right minds wants war, whatever their nationality or creed.

It might sound like stating the obvious, but peace is not simply the cessation of war. Peace depends on continually addressing the causes of war: poverty and injustice, ruthless political ambition, territorial expansion, financial manipulation, and the desire for power. It seems to me that it is also a matter of education, of teaching people that to settle an argument by violence is a primitive and wasteful approach to problem solving.

Can we ever hope for a day when war will no longer exist? Or do we believe, as previous generations have believed, that war is both natural and inevitable? Well, things do change. In our legal system we have not always had 'trial by jury'. Curiously, 'trial by jury' was preceded by 'trial by ordeal and combat'. Even after the jury system was introduced there was a period when it was legal to settle differences by duelling with pistols or swords. Thank heavens that dunking women in ponds to test them for witchcraft, or legally shooting people with whom we have a difference is no longer considered the best approach. The jury system, although not perfect, is a huge improvement on trial by ordeal or combat, but at some point there had to be a commitment on someone's part to develop a new system that eventually replaced the old.

Duelling was once considered noble and honourable. Today most people would see it as primitive, stupid, unreliable and unjust. So let us pray for the day when war and battles are no longer seen as the 'right' way to solve differences, but as stupid, wasteful and evil.

Eternal God,
cleanse our hearts from the envy, fear and
*   ignorance*
that breeds conflict and strife; give us
*   instead the courage,*
wisdom and will to build a world of love
*   and peace,*
in the name of the Prince of Peace, even
*   Jesus Christ our Lord.*
Amen.

Private prayer list

Some people have told me that when they say their prayers in private, they start well enough but, before they know were they are, their minds have wandered off down all sorts of interesting avenues, and they don't feel they are really praying. Actually I wouldn't worry about that too much. In ordinary conversation it's very easy to go off at a tangent, and I'm sure the Holy Spirit can interpret our meanderings just as well as our so-called 'ordered' thoughts.

There is one possible answer to the wandering or perhaps forgetful mind and that is to make a prayer list. I was once privileged to see a most beautiful prayer list that belonged to an elderly lady I used to visit. At first glance it looked like a little photograph album. Each page was covered with small photographs. Sometimes it was a complete picture and sometimes a tiny head and shoulders that had been carefully cut from a snapshot. By each picture was a name and sometimes a date, such as a birthday that she wanted to remember.

Then, further on, the photographs were replaced by a simple list of names. She had also written out some of her favourite prayers for easy reference. I remember being very moved by the care she had taken in making her prayer list. It was a private and beautiful work of art, a little jewel which I am sure was valued not only by the owner but also by God.

For most of us a notebook would be the easiest thing to use. The name and address pages or 'notes' pages at the back of your diary could be used for your prayer list, or perhaps you could use your mobile phone directory of numbers as your list. Either would ensure that your prayer list is near at hand.

It need not take a long time to pray your prayer list. You need only bring each person before God by name, perhaps praying particularly for those who are sick or who are going through a difficult time, or who have asked to be remembered in your prayers. Remembering people before God may do a number of things for the one who prays. If, like my friend, you write down birthdays, then you are not likely to forget those important dates. In addition you may be prompted to write a letter, or make a telephone call or visit someone on your list. At the heart of your praying is the thought that, through the mystery of prayer, the person you have named might, at that moment, somehow enjoy the peace of the knowledge of the presence of God. Sometimes, friends and relatives, husbands and wives, parents and children who are perhaps temporarily separated can unite in prayer by agreeing to pray together at a particular time every day. It is a good way of being spiritually close to someone you love who is far away.

Father,
as I remember those I love in prayer,
fill them with your Spirit and your love.
And wherever they may be at this moment
may they know and enjoy the peace of
*   your presence.*
Amen.

Promises, promises

In the great Gershwin musical *Porgy and Bess*, there is a wonderful song that says, 'The things that you're li'ble to read in the Bible, It ain't necessarily so'. This is a very profound statement. Many of the stories in the Bible are simply vehicles for teaching us a truth or raising a question in our minds.

I came across a modern humorous version of the story of Noah and the building of the ark:

> The Lord said unto Noah, 'Where is the ark I commanded you to build?' and Noah answered, 'Verily, I have three carpenters off sick. The gopher wood supplier hath let me down – yea, even though the gopher wood hath been on order for nigh upon twelve months, and the damp-course specialist hath not turned up.'

> And God said to Noah, 'I want the ark finished before seven days and seven nights.' Noah said, 'It will be so.' But it was not so.

> The Lord said to Noah, 'What seemeth to be the trouble this time?'

> Noah said, 'My sub-contractor hath gone bankrupt. The pitch for the outside of the ark hath not arrived and the glazier hath

departed on holiday to Majorca, yea, even though I offered him double time.'

The Lord grew angry and said, 'What about the animals? Two of every sort I have ordered to be kept alive. Where, for example, are the giraffes?'

And Noah said, 'They have been delivered to the wrong address, but should arrive by Friday.'

And the Lord said to Noah, 'Where are the monkeys, and the elephants and the zebras?' Noah said, 'They are expected today.'

The Lord said, 'How about the unicorns?' Noah wrung his hands and wept. 'O Lord, they are a discontinued line. Thou canst not get unicorns for love nor money. Thou knowest how it is.'

And the Lord said, 'Noah, my son, I know. Why else dost thou think I sent a flood?'

I suppose the point of this version of the story is that it's no good making promises unless you intend to keep them. Simply talking about doing something is not a lot of good, it's actually doing it that counts.

Jesus once said, 'Not everybody who says, "Lord, Lord" will enter the kingdom, but those who do the will of God, they will enter my Father's kingdom.' In other words, don't make promises. Don't just talk about justice and peace and mercy, but do it. And that's the problem for most of us. We know what we ought to do; it's actually doing it that's difficult.

*Loving, patient God, whose promises are
    fulfilled
in and through your Son, Jesus Christ,
forgive our failure to live up to our
    promises,
our selfish and inward-looking attitudes,
our attempts to avoid responsibility
for the hungry, the poor and homeless.
Fill us with your compassion
that, seeing the need and distress
of sisters and brothers throughout the
    world,
our words of commitment may translate
    into deeds
of mercy and love, offered in the name of
    your Son,
our Lord and Saviour. Amen.*

Resolutions

I couldn't add up the number of years I have been making and breaking New Year resolutions. I can't count the things I have been going to do, or the good intentions I failed to do. So this year, instead of drawing up a list of honourable intentions and brave resolutions, perhaps I should make a list of all the things I am *not* going to do in the New Year:

1. I am *not* going to diet. I am now convinced that dieting makes you fat!

2. I am *not* going to count calories or eat things that have labels that say: 'This product can only help you slim when it is part of a calorie controlled diet'. I mean, you could stick that label on anything, couldn't you? Christmas *puddings* will only help you slim when they are part of a calorie controlled diet! No. I am going to eat anything I like – but *less* of it, half of it, perhaps? And here is another 'Not' resolution:

3. I am *not* going to clear my plate, although it was drilled into me as a child that I was only a 'good boy' if I did. Strapped into my high-chair they would only release me when they could say, 'There's a good boy! All gone!' Perhaps I'll just put less on the plate in the first place.

Actually, I've just realized why the Ten Commandments work as a set of rules for the majority of us

'Thou shalt not' is somehow far more bearable than the positive, 'You will'. There is something slightly unacceptable about 'You *will* be good – you *will* be kind and generous, you *will* tell the truth'. Perhaps that's why I like these 'not' resolutions. Let's see, what else am I *not* going to do?

4. I am *not* going to screech *'You raving lunatic!'* the next time someone cuts me up on the North Circular Road. I shall just take a deep breath and say, 'Such suffering, such stress, such pain. God bless you, friend!'

And that's another thing I'm *not* going to do:

5. I'm *not* going to drive along the North Circular Road!

6. I'm definitely *not* going to watch any more late-night movies, for two good reasons: they're on too late, there are very few good ones and – I've seen them all. Actually, that three good reasons!

7. I am certainly *not* going to ask anyone again for road directions, I'll buy a map. I am convinced that terminal brain damage will set in if I hear someone say, just once more, 'You take the second left after the Black Horse, no, I tell a lie – it's the Dun Cow.'

But come to think of it, when Jesus reduced the *Ten* Commandments to *one* new law, it wasn't negative, but very positive: 'A new commandment I give you: love one another, as I have loved you.' Now *that* would be a good New Year resolution.

Now where was I with that list of 'nots'?

8. I am definitely *not* going to buy an exercise bike . . .

9. . . . or a rowing machine . . .

10. . . . and certainly not a skipping rope.

I'm just going to walk tall and *think* thin.

> *Lord,*
> *help me to stop thinking about the future,*
> *to enjoy the present moment,*
> *to devote each day*
> *to loving those I have been given to love,*
> *and to remember*
> *that I am always in your presence.*
> *Amen.*

Rule of life

In 1720, when John Wesley was a 17-year-old student in his first year at Oxford, he was given £30 to live on for the year. He managed to get by on £28, so he gave what he had saved, £2, to the poor. The next year, receiving £60, he still lived on £28, so gave away £32. The third year he received £90, and gave away £62. The fourth year he received £120. Still he lived on £28, and he gave the poor all the rest.

That story of John Wesley as a student reveals an awareness of the poor and a responsibility towards them which was to set a pattern for the rest of his life. Of course, he did not simply spend his life handing out money to the poor. Later he used both effort and ingenuity to find ways of helping people to escape the poverty trap.

One way out was through education. But there were no free schools. Some parents managed to scrape together enough money to buy a very basic education, although in many of the schools, as John Wesley discovered, the children learned all kinds of vice as well. He was so appalled by what was happening to the children, he decided to take action:

> At length I determined to have them taught
> in my own house that they might have an
> opportunity of learning to read, write,

and cast accounts (if no more), without being under almost a necessity of learning Heathenism at the same time. And after several unsuccessful trials, I found two such schoolmasters as I wanted, men of honesty and of sufficient knowledge, who had talents for, and their hearts in, the work. They have now under their care nearly sixty children.

The parents of some pay for their schooling; but the greater part, being very poor, do not; so that the expense is chiefly defrayed by voluntary contributions. We have of late clothed them too, as many as wanted.

That school set up in John Wesley's house was the beginning of his work in educating the poor. At the end of the nineteenth century, before there was any such thing as free state education, there were more than 1,000 Methodist day schools in England.

Wesley once wrote a rule for Christian living which in many ways sums up his life and work:

> Do all the good you can,
> by all the means you can,
> in all the ways you can,
> in all the places you can,
> at all the times you can
> to all people you can,
> as long as ever you can.

Few people could live such an intensely dedicated life, but let's thank God for those whose commitment and self-sacrifice has enriched us all.

Lord Christ,
You have no body on earth but ours,
No hands but ours,
No feet but ours.
Ours are the eyes through which your
    compassion
Must look out on the world.
Ours are the hands with which
You bless people now.
Bless our minds and bodies,
That we may be a blessing to others.
Amen.

St Teresa of Avila (1515–82)

'Secular vicars'

When Tony Blair was Prime Minister he spoke of the need for 'secular vicars', people who would be willing to teach ethics and morality, draw up guidelines of what is and what isn't acceptable behaviour and practice in business, in the workplace, in the shops and on the streets.

'Hang on,' you might say, 'isn't that what the Church should be doing?' And the answer is yes, but sadly the Church doesn't seem to be communicating with so many people these days. And again you might ask, 'Why?'

In the days when 'missionaries' took their faith to other lands the first thing they had to do was to learn the language of the country. Not long ago, I heard a Church of England clergyman say, jokingly, 'I speak Anglican, and to truly understand us you need to understand the Anglican language.' Now, he was joking but, in my view, part of the failure of the Church today is that it isn't speaking the same language as the people.

Others might say, 'Surely, ethics and morality ought to be taught in our schools?' That's not so easy either. We are a multicultural society which, hopefully, respects other cultures. Teachers may not try to persuade their pupils to a particular religious point of view, so religious ethics can only be taught academically. Well, there's not a lot of 'fire' in that. To teach something with conviction it helps if you actually believe it, and are allowed to teach it with some passion.

Who are the best 'secular vicars' likely to be? Well, historically, our law and culture is based on biblical teaching from the Ten Commandments to the Sermon on the Mount, so the best teachers are likely to be those who have thought or prayed, studied, discussed and argued about what is right or wrong, or good and true, and who have also decided to live according to their convictions. I don't mean priests, ministers and lawyers, I mean people of integrity in every walk of life, principally, people who are 'in the world'.

It is they who are called upon to take a stand in the workplace, to do business in a manner that is compatible with the beliefs on which our society is founded. There would undoubtedly be catcalls and howls of 'holier than thou' if our 'secular vicars' were simply to 'preach' in the workplace. If, however, we want a society that puts people before profits, that believes in building up a sense of community rather than a culture of 'What's in it for me?' then those who believe these things will need to learn the language of the street and stand up and be counted, not so much in what they say as in what they do. It won't be easy, but then again, it never has been.

> *Jesus, friend, brother and guide,*
> *whose experience embraces mockery and*
>   *rejection,*
> *fill us with your grace and courage,*
> *that our lives may bear witness*
> *to your life-enhancing love of all that is good,*
> *true, honourable and eternal,*
> *for your name's sake. Amen.*

Siesta – time to think

When one of our sons, Simon, lived and worked for a number of years in Argentina we visited him, his wife Jane and their children, one of whom had been born there, several times.

Tropical South America has very hot summers, which always brings to my mind Noel Coward's famous song, 'Mad Dogs and Englishmen go out in the Midday Sun'. He was talking about the fact that, in tropical countries the world over, at the hottest time of day people take a siesta. Unless, of course, you are English.

During one of our visits, while driving towards Paraguay and Brazil, we developed a problem with the car. So we pulled off the main road into the first little town indicated by a lop-sided sign. It was hardly a town: dirt-track roads, dust-covered adobe buildings. It was hot and still except for the buzz of flies and the clicking of cicadas. However, there was a petrol station where we found a slumbering man who directed us to a house where there was a mechanic. We knocked at the door of the mechanic's house and eventually, after some interior bumps and footsteps, the door opened a crack, and a woman's face appeared. She squinted at us suspiciously.

'Buenos dias, Senor.'

'Buenos dias, Senora.'

We asked her, 'Was this the house of the mechanic?'

'Si, Senor, pero es la hora de la *siesta*!'

('Yes, Senor, but it is the hour of s*iesta*!')

Whilst we struggled to find a reply to this indisputable fact, she looked at us with utter disbelief, and then, without a word, shut the door.

Until now, we had spent most of our time in cities or big towns where the concept of siesta had declined, but we were now deep in the vast and remote countryside of the Pampas. Here siesta was a period of time which could not be disturbed, even (or especially) by an Englishman or a mad dog. It was my first lesson in the cultural need to respect the siesta, to respect people's need for a time of quiet, of stillness. So whether we liked it or not we had to wait, to find a shady place and be still.

The curious thing was that in this quiet time, when we stopped fretting about 'getting on', stopped worrying about what time it was, and just sat still, it suddenly became absolutely clear to me what was wrong with the car and what we had to do. In Argentina, I learned that a compulsory 'siesta' every day is a good idea.

> *Lord,*
> *teach me to be still,*
> *to 'siesta' in your presence*
> *at least once this day;*
> *and in that time of stillness*
> *to discover your peace,*
> *the peace which passes understanding.*
> *Amen.*

Speaking the truth in love

John Wesley, who with his brother Charles founded the first Methodist 'societies', was convinced that Christians ought always to be able to 'speak the truth in love' to each other, something that is far more difficult than it sounds.

Wesley wanted people to try to live as closely as possible to the teachings of Jesus Christ, and one of the things that Jesus taught was that we should love our enemies as well as our friends. Wesley was involved in a great deal of controversy throughout his life, and he made enemies wherever he went. He and the early Methodists were often physically attacked and publicly reviled. On a number of occasions Wesley himself, who was only about five-foot-three and very thin, had to face hired thugs who had been sent to break up his meetings. He was knocked to the ground, twice dragged by his hair, and twice escaped the mob by swimming across rivers. But whenever he was confronted by danger, his first response was not to run but to face his adversaries and to 'speak the truth in love' to them. And very often it worked.

On one occasion he was in a house when a mob, armed with sticks and cudgels, started shouting and demanding that Wesley be sent outside to them. Suddenly the ringleader burst into the house with several others. To everyone's amazement Wesley immediately walked up to him, smiled and asked, 'What evil have I done? Which of you have I wronged?' Then turning to the others he said, 'Have I ever wronged you? Or you? Or you?'

In the silence that followed he said, 'My chief offence appears to be that I offer the love of God to any who will listen.' Not only did they listen but the ringleader of the mob, a well known prize-fighter, was so won over that he acted as Wesley's bodyguard as he walked through the crowd. Later he became a Methodist himself and a staunch defender of Methodism until he died some 45 years later.

Relationships between Catholics and Protestants in Wesley's day were not at all friendly, yet in a letter to a Catholic priest, perhaps quoting from his own sermon on 'The Catholic Spirit', Wesley wrote: 'Though we cannot think alike, may we not love alike? May we be of one heart, though we are not of one opinion? If in our common love of Christ your heart is as my heart, then give me your hand.' When he says 'may we be of one heart', Wesley does not mean that we should be of the same opinion, or embrace the same style of worship, or agree on the same form of ecclesiastical government or choose extempore prayer as opposed to written prayer. Instead, he wanted a relationship of the heart, one that puts aside opinion in favour of natural, heartfelt feelings. A love of God and the human race was all that was needed. Then, and then only, did he feel that he could 'speak the truth in love'.

> *O God of truth and love, we ask forgiveness for those times when our opinions have prevented us from loving, or our 'way of doing things' has caused division. Teach us to*

speak the truth with your love, the love that forgives, heals and reconciles in the name of Jesus Christ, our Lord and Saviour.
Amen.

Speaking through us

I attended a Church synod meeting where we discussed the joys and difficulties of being a minister. One of the difficulties that every pastoral minister experiences is a feeling of deep inadequacy, the feeling that we are not up to the job, not good enough, wise enough, or quick-witted enough to respond satisfactorily to people's needs as they present themselves.

I can't count the number of times I have set off in fear and trepidation, thinking, 'What can I do? What can I say in this situation? What have I to offer this man, this woman, or what comfort can I offer this family in this particular situation?' And time and time again, I have found myself standing on someone's doorstep, saying to myself these words from Matthew: 'Do not worry about what you are to speak or what you are to say; for what you are to say will be given to you at that time; for it is not you who speak, but the Spirit of your Father speaking through you' (Matt. 10.19–20).

Every time, it is not that I have risen to the occasion, but that the Holy Spirit has used the occasion to speak to those in need 'through' me. That is one of the huge privileges of ministry, and it is not confined merely to those who are ordained, but extends to everyone who is called upon to minister to others. It has nothing to do with our spirituality or lack of it; it is enough to say, 'Here am I, Lord, if you can use me, then here I am.'

Many times I have 'felt in my bones' that I should call on someone. Often the thought only occurs as I am driving past the end of their road. Then, suddenly, I find my hand on the doorbell and I listen to someone saying, 'How did you know? I was just gong to ring you.'

In the past, people have said to me, 'I wish I could do something, but I wouldn't know what to say. I wouldn't have the right words, I haven't had any training. I'd be tongue-tied.' The answer to that problem is, I think, is in those words from Matthew. I usually adapt it into a little doorstep prayer:

Lord, I have nothing to say,
unless you speak through me.
In your mercy, be in my head
and on my lips.

Very few of us think of ourselves as brave, as the stuff of saints and martyrs. Usually we would rather not see, hear or speak. Our natural inclination is probably to turn away. Most of us would like a quiet, undisturbed life. But the dilemma lies in the fact that we cannot love God and ignore the needs of those around us. We need to pray for confidence, not necessarily to be counsellors or givers of advice, but simply to be the bearers of God's comfort and love.

Lord,
I have no strength but your strength,
no wisdom but your wisdom,
no words worth hearing
unless you speak.
Lord, in that hour,
be in my mind and on my lips.
Amen.

Strewth, cor lummie and saints alive!

It is perhaps surprising how many religious ideas and concepts are disguised in the language we use day by day. 'You're an absolute angel,' we say, if someone has done something unexpectedly kind, or, 'Be an angel,' we say, when we want someone to do us a favour.

Even expletives have their origin in religious language and thought. 'Strewth!' somebody might say, rarely being aware that they are using an abbreviation of 'God's truth'. Similarly the word, 'lummie', as in, 'Cor lummie, Gov', a phrase frequently on the lips of Cockney characters in old British 'B' movies, is derived from 'God, love me'.

People have sometimes describe a very helpful individual as 'a saint'. To some the word 'saint' means a man or woman who has been canonized by the Church and given the word 'saint' as a title, like St Peter or St Paul. In many traditional works of art, you can recognize the 'saints' by the white or golden halo hovering over their heads. But when St Paul, writing to the church at Corinth, sends greetings to 'all the saints', he does not mean all the people who have been canonized, because canonization hadn't been invented. So what did he mean?

Paul was a Jew, and there is a concept of 'saints' in Judaism. In the Old Testament of the Bible there are frequent references to saints, which might come as a bit of a surprise to those who assumed that the word 'saint' was a Christian word. The Hebrew word which has been translated as 'saints' is 'Hasidim'. The Hasidim were godly, prayerful people whose saintliness was revealed chiefly through their kindness to others.

Paul was also unable to use the word 'Christian' when writing to the Corinthian church, since the word was not in general use at that time. So instead he writes to the 'saints'.

In churches and cathedrals, 'saints' are portrayed in huge stained-glass images, and they all seem to belong to a medieval stained-glass world that is completely removed from the world in which we live. At least I used to think so, until I heard a story of a child who, standing in front of a stained-glass window in a magnificent cathedral, asked:

'Who are those people with white rings floating over their heads?'

'They are the saints,' was the reply.

'What,' asked the child, 'is a saint?'

There was a slight pause, and the person put on the spot, as we so often are by the simple and direct questions of children, replied, 'Saints, are – er – people through whom the light shines.'

Actually, that is not a bad answer. I like that definition of a saint: 'someone through whom the light shines'. In fact, I can think of one or two people who fit that description rather well, and they are neither

'stained-glass' people nor canonized by the Church.
But I think they are 'saints' in my book.

> *Loving God, whose angels proclaimed the
> saving name of Mary's child, grant that
> we may live each day in the light of your
> incarnate love, and may that same light
> shine through our lives to the glory of your
> name.*
> *Amen.*

Survival rules

When I was a teacher, we used a role-play game in class when we studied the rules and laws of society. The class divided into small groups and each had to imagine that they were a committee representing the survivors of a disaster that had wiped out most of the world's population.

Across the world there were small pockets of survivors. But none of our sophisticated services were functioning. No factories, police forces, armies; no oil, gas or power. There were supplies of food in various warehouses but there was no food industry to provide more when the supplies ran out. It was as if the world was starting all over again. Each 'survival committee' had to work out what they ought to do for the continuing good of the survivors.

Would they ration the food? Who would be in charge of rationing? How would they stop the strong stealing from the weak? How would they protect themselves? Who would look after the old, the young and the vulnerable?

I would 'stir the pot' from time to time by sending messages to the groups; for example, 'Some children have got into a brewery and have made themselves ill by drinking. What will you do? Destroy the brewery? Lock it up? Guard it? Teach the children about the dangers of alcohol? What?'

By the end of the role play each group had drawn up a list of things they believed necessary for people to survive. Most groups, in one way or another, had decided that they had to face up to reality, to be honest and accurate in the assessment of their situation. So getting at the truth and telling the truth was very important.

Work had to begin immediately, whether it was farming, fishing or organizing their resources. Stealing could not be tolerated. Violence had to be curbed. The young, the vulnerable and the elderly had to be cared for and treated with respect.

In the last quarter of the lesson I would ask them to read from the Bible, Exodus 20. There they would find a group of survivors, who had escaped from slavery and spent 40 years in a wild and barbaric environment, and who had also drawn up a set of 'rules for survival'. They too had arrived at the conclusion that to survive you could not allow people to steal, or kill or show no respect for the elderly, and that life became intolerable if people lied or distorted the truth. These 'rules' were, of course, the Ten Commandments. Generations later, Jesus, who was descended from these same people, revealed that the greatest of the commandments was to love God and to love your neighbour as yourself.

> *Gracious Lord and Father of us all, you have taught us, through your Son, Jesus Christ, that the greatest commandment is to love God and our neighbours as ourselves. In your mercy teach us how to live not by law, but by love.*
> *Amen.*

Thank you, for everything

As children we were taught that the most special words we had to use were 'please' and 'thank you'. You never asked for anything without saying 'please' and whenever you were given something, 'thank you' was the first thing you said. We were taught that it was polite to say thank you after a birthday party, to say thank you for a Christmas present, to thank God for the food we were about to eat. Sometimes we would sing our 'thank you':

> Thank you for the world so sweet,
> Thank you for the food we eat,
> Thank you for the birds that sing,
> Thank you, God, for everything.

For some reason, when we grow up, saying 'thank you' is not always so automatic. Perhaps we become less alert to the things for which we should be thankful. Perhaps children are more alert, more alive, more excited by far more things than grown-ups – wriggling worms, tadpoles growing legs, caterpillars under leaves – things that grown-ups no longer even notice. Ask yourself, truthfully, when was the last time you saw a tadpole? When was the last time you 'squealed with delight' at anything? And if we are not alert or sensitive to what is going on around us, are we in danger of not 'living' so much as simply 'existing'?

To a child the world is an exciting, exhilarating, scary place to be explored and enjoyed. If being grown-up means losing our sense of wonder then perhaps that is what Jesus meant when he said that unless we 'become as little children' we will never be able to enter the kingdom of heaven.

I'm beginning to think that 'gratitude' is one of the keys to living in heaven. After all, a 'squeal of delight' *is* an expression of gratitude. To be able to live thankfully is, I think, to be truly alive. It means the difference between drifting aimlessly through our days and savouring and enjoying all the things for which we can be grateful.

I don't think I truly began to understand the full implications of our childhood song, 'Thank you, God, for *everything*', until I met a blind woman named Adele Dafesh. She was the headmistress of a school for the blind in North Africa. She came from a very poor Arab village and had lost her sight as a child. As a result, she was sent to a special school where she did well; she was sent from there to college, where she achieved a degree and became a teacher. She became an international ambassador for the poor and the blind, founding schools and bringing a vision of hope to thousands of people.

I asked her if she ever felt bitter about losing her sight. Her reply astonished me. She said, 'No. I thank God for my blindness. Blindness took me out of that poor village, took me to college, opened up a whole world that I would never have experienced if I had not lost my sight. Instead of "eyesight", I was given a vision, which I have not yet finished exploring.'

More than anyone I have ever met, or perhaps ever will meet, Adele Dafesh was someone who really understood the meaning of 'living thankfully'.

> *God most Holy, Spirit of love and*
> *generosity,*
> *who gives meaning to our lives,*
> *fill our hearts and minds with gratitude,*
> *that we may spend our days*
> *in grateful celebration of the mystery of*
> *your bounty*
> *by reflecting your love in our lives.*
> *Amen.*

Thanks for the memory

During a family holiday, one of our sons, Mark, said, 'I keep telling myself to remember to record some "golden moments" in my mind, you know, to stop, and drink in everything about the place we're in, the people we meet and the things we are doing, and to fix them in my head, label them, as pictures to remember.'

Psychiatrists say that everything we see, hear or experience is recorded in our memories. The memory is like a huge computer, and the things we experience are stored deep inside. Some say that the equation for defining our individual personality is 'the sum of all our experiences divided by how we dealt with them'.

Of course, to be complete human beings we have to know how to deal with the bad things as well as the good. When bad things do happen that's when our knowledge and experience of goodness and love stand us in good stead, another reason why we need to store up happy, positive experiences. The 'trick' of a good memory is being able to label things so that you can find them when you want them and recall them easily.

Once, at the Edinburgh Festival Fringe, I performed three full-length one-man shows in rotation, two performances each day, throughout the entire three weeks of the festival. It meant carrying in my mind more than four hours of remembered texts. I was frequently asked, as many actors are, 'How on earth do you remember all your lines?' The answer is that you have to make 'labels', mental 'signposts' that lead you from one idea to the next. To keep these signposts in the front of your mind you have to rehearse them and repeat them so often that the moment a signpost flips up it immediately points to a particular arrangement of words.

This is why we need to 'rehearse' the good things in our lives, to tell the familiar stories of laughter and love over and over, so that we live with positive signposts in our minds. Paul, in his letter to the Philippians said:

> Whatever is true, whatever is honourable, whatever is just, whatever is pure, whatever is pleasing, whatever is commendable, if there is any excellence and if there is anything worthy of praise, think about these things. Keep on doing the things you have learned and received and heard and seen in me, and the God of peace will be with you.
>
> Phil. 4.8–9

Loving Lord, fill our minds and enrich our memories with those things that are true and right and lovely that our thoughts may be generous, our actions kind, and our days inspired by the knowledge of your love, through Jesus Christ our Lord.
Amen.

The authority of love

In the city of Bristol, outside the Corn Exchange, there are on the pavement some curious lumps of stone that look a bit like bird tables. In fact they are called 'The Nails', because it was on 'nails' like these that, in the past, great commercial deals were struck and payments would be made in cash. This is where the expression 'paying on the nail' comes from.

Of course, before anyone can say, 'OK, it's a deal' and shake hands on it, they have to have the authority to spend vast amounts of money, to close the deal themselves. The story in Luke's Gospel (Lk. 7.1–10) about the healing of a Roman officer's servant, is a wonderful example of someone recognizing authority in another person.

The Roman officer was, as he said, a man who was able to say, 'Go' to people under him and they went; 'Do this' and they did it. However, this particular Roman officer also knew a great deal about people. He had clearly won the friendship and support of the local population. He had taken an interest in their religion, found out what they believed, and had even built a synagogue for them.

He knew about military authority, but he also knew about moral and spiritual authority. He knew about the carpenter of Nazareth – either he had gone out of his way to hear Jesus himself speak, or he had made a point of finding out about his teaching, because without doubt he had learned or seen in Jesus the spiritual authority that healed and restored people. And so he says to Jesus, with complete confidence, 'Sir, just give the order, and my servant will be healed.'

Jesus is surprised and says that he has never met faith like this before. Now, the interesting thing is that there is no mention in the story of Jesus saying any healing words. The story says simply that when the messengers returned to the Roman's house, they found that his servant was healed. So Jesus didn't even have to say the word; he had only to think – and healing happened.

Recognition of the spiritual authority and power of Jesus is contained in the prayer that is an adaptation of the Roman officer's words: 'Lord, say but the word and my soul shall be healed.'

If we have the same faith and confidence in Jesus as the Roman officer had, and if we call on Jesus to heal our souls, then in that moment we are forgiven, the burden of our guilt is removed and we are at peace with God. That is the authority of Jesus, the power to forgive and to restore, now, at this very moment.

> *Lord Jesus, yours is the authority of love, love that defeats evil with goodness, that comforts the distressed and brings peace to those who pray, 'Lord, in your mercy, say but the word, and we shall be healed.'*
> *Amen.*

The essential you

I saw a programme on television about that much loved and respected actor, the late Sir John Mills. At the time of making the programme he was 88, hard of hearing and with very little eyesight, but somehow he seemed to be, essentially, the same John Mills we had always known, with the same modesty and reticence, the same honesty and humour, almost the same youthfulness. Then I remembered reading an anonymous philosophical reflection that said: 'Youth is not so much a time of life, as a state of mind' or, as the old chestnut has it, 'You're as old as you feel'.

The writer argued that nobody grows old merely by living a particular number of years. Real ageing begins with your first cynical thought, with the first surrender of an ideal or a dream. Years might wrinkle your skin but real ageing is to do with the wrinkles in your soul. And the things that wrinkle your soul? Well, they are things like guilt, particularly the guilt we bury deep inside because we can't deal with it, face it and forgive ourselves.

We are also aged on the inside by things over which we have no control: disappointments, worry, fear, betrayals of friendship. It is how we deal with such setbacks, however, that can affect our inner ageing. If worries and disappointments or failures can be seen instead as learning experiences, or if we can reduce the number of our worries by putting aside those things about which we can do nothing, then we can reduce their effect on us.

When I was a student I remember a particular tutor who was always saying, 'Of course, when you get to my age . . . '. He clearly thought of himself as an old man even though he was quite a few years away from retirement. Among my fellow-students at that time were several mature students, not very different in age from the tutor who was weighed down by his years. They felt that going back to studying in their mature years was positively rejuvenating. Age, it seems, is sometimes 'in the mind'.

Like them, we also might be able to counter the effects of inner ageing by keeping alive our appetite for learning, by never entirely losing faith or hope, and never ceasing to love people or life itself. That anonymous passage I recalled earlier ended by saying:

> You are as young as your faith, as old as
> your doubt;
> as young as your self-confidence. as old as
> your fear;
> as young as your hope, as old as your
> despair.

We could make up our own list:

> You are as old as your prejudices, as young
> as your generosity.
> You are as old as your hatred and as young
> as your love for the world and your
> neighbour.
> You are as old as the grudges you hold and
> as young as your ability to forgive and
> forget.

Loving Lord,
in whose sight a thousand years
is but the twinkling of an eye,
keep our spirits fresh and alive
through faith in you,
hope for the world
and love for our neighbour, for Christ's
    sake.
Amen.

The pilgrim spirit

Whit Sunday and Bank Holiday Whit Monday are both derived from the word 'white'. Originally Whit Sunday was called 'white' Sunday, as it was a popular day for baptisms, when those to be baptized wore white. Nowadays it is known as Pentecost, and the Bank Holiday has been separated from it and renamed the Spring Bank Holiday.

It was on this day that the disciples of Jesus received the Holy Spirit. It was an exciting and strange event: people heard a sound like a mighty wind, and saw what looked like tongues of flame resting on the heads of the disciples. Then, perhaps strangest of all, the disciples began to speak to a crowd of people – pilgrims to Jerusalem from all over the world – and each person heard what was being said in their own language.

That used to sound strange to me, until I became involved in religious broadcasting. Over the years I have received many letters thanking me for saying things which I knew I had not actually said. I was saying one thing, but it seemed that some people were hearing another. Eventually I realized that there are times when the Holy Spirit speaks to people's hearts and minds through other people's words, and I was humbled that my broadcasts had become a channel of the Holy Spirit, an instrument of peace.

The story in the Acts of the Apostles tells us that when the disciples received the Holy Spirit, more than 3,000 people were convinced by their message and baptized. As many of them were from different parts of the world, they took their new-found faith with them when they returned home, and the pilgrim Church had begun.

I was reading a book the other day by Gerard Hughes, who said that the Church was 'of its nature, a pilgrim church, a questioning and learning church', and that the whole of one's life should also be a questioning and learning pilgrimage.

Of course, it is not easy, because, like John Bunyan's Pilgrim, we find the way is strewn with obstacles and horrible 'sloughs of despond'. There is a great temptation to stop in a comfortable place and say, 'This is it. Here's the truth, there's no need to go any further', and to close our minds to disturbing questions, to issues that demand we keep on searching for answers and solutions. But the true 'pilgrim spirit', the Holy Spirit, is the very opposite of the closed mind. As Gerard Hughes says, 'The Spirit of God is a spirit of love, of truth and openness.'

> *Lead us, Lord,*
> *on our pilgrimage;*
> *from darkness to light,*
> *from falsehood to truth,*
> *from conflict to peace,*
> *from anger to love,*
> *and from sadness to joy.*
> *Amen.*

True-grit pilgrim

In *True Grit*, one of the Western movies that starred John Wayne, his character, Rooster Cogburn, greeted strangers by saying, in Wayne's unmistakable drawl, 'Well, hello, pilgrim.'

I like the association of the words 'true grit' and 'pilgrim', because they suggest the kind of courage that is needed to make any pilgrimage. In June 2000 a group of people made a pilgrimage from Birmingham to Cologne, a walk of some 410 miles called the Jubilee 2000 Debt March. They were walking to draw attention to the terrible plight of some of the poorest countries in the world and they walked for 20 days, averaging about 20 miles a day. It was a gruelling walk, which involved blisters, near exhaustion and a great deal of, well, 'true grit'.

In 563, St Columba set out on a missionary pilgrimage, accompanied by 12 monks, from Ireland to Scotland. The only boat available to them was an open coracle. Crossing the Irish Sea in an open boat is a hazardous voyage in any century, but in the year 563, with no navigational aids and no rescue system of any kind, I think it must have required a fair amount of 'true grit'. There is a prayer of St Columba which suggests that travelling anywhere in those days was an anxious occupation:

Alone with none but thee, my God,
I journey on my way.
What need I fear, when thou art near,
O King of night and day?
More safe am I, within thy hand,
than if a host did round me stand.

St Columba and his monks made it across the Irish
Sea in their coracle and landed on the Isle of Iona
where they founded one of the most celebrated mon-
asteries in Britain. The Celtic monks had a wonderful
collection of pilgrim or travelling prayers – here's one
that might have been said on St Columba's boat, or
even on the Debt March to Cologne.

May the road rise up to meet you,
May the wind be always at your back,
May the sun shine warm upon your face,
May the rain fall soft upon your fields,
And, until we meet again,
May God hold you
In the palm of his hand.
Amen.

Two good men and true

In 2003, the 300th anniversary of the birth of John Wesley, one of the founders of Methodism, was celebrated. Wesley spent a great number of years in what were the 'mean streets' of the city of London, not far from St Paul's Cathedral, where pickpockets and rogues of every description slipped in and out of the dark alleys which housed brothels and infamous 'thieves' kitchens'.

Not far away, just off Fleet Street, was the home of Wesley's friend, Dr Samuel Johnson. Dr Johnson was born in Lichfield in 1709. At the age of 28, after an unsuccessful attempt to become a schoolmaster, he set out for London, determined to make a living as a writer. It was a terrible struggle. His early days in London were so poverty-stricken that when he was reminded of them years later, he burst into tears. Working as a theatre critic and essayist, he gradually became known to publishers and booksellers. One of them, Robert Dodsley, suggested that Johnson should write a dictionary.

It took Johnson eight years to write the dictionary, so it did not exactly free him from his money worries, but in the end the dictionary brought him fame and doctorates from Dublin and Oxford Universities. Ultimately, his poverty was relieved when the Government awarded him a pension of £300 a year.

Dr Johnson was a brilliant conversationalist whose witticisms were quoted throughout the fashionable society of his day, but he never forgot his days of poverty. He was a man of faith and his convictions guided his daily living. Samuel Johnson was deeply compassionate towards the poor; a generous almsgiver, he frequently took needy people into his own home. His friend, John Wesley, had the same concern. Wesley founded societies called the 'The Stranger's Friend' which were committed to helping the poor or the stranger in distress, both practically and financially. When asked, 'Who qualifies for this help?' he said, 'The *only* test is need.'

Wesley spoke out against the slave trade at a time when much of the wealth in Britain relied on slave-based estates in the West Indies and America. He and his brother Charles believed they had a mission to bring England, and the Church of England, back to the principles of scriptural holiness. The attempt proved very costly to them personally. They were persecuted, suffered physical violence, mockery and abuse from their contemporaries, but nevertheless continued with their mission to the end of their lives.

Both Wesley and Johnson, in their different ways, echoed in their lives the teachings of Jesus in the story of the Good Samaritan, in which Jesus said, 'Love God with all your mind, with all your heart and with all your strength, and love your neighbour as yourself.' And when asked, 'Who is my neighbour?' he answered obliquely with a story which asked another question: 'Which of the people in this story would you consider to be a good neighbour?' The answer is clear: if you see someone in need, don't ask what nationality they are, or what religion, or what race, or whether they can pay you back, just meet their need as generously as you can.

Dr Johnson and John Wesley were good talkers; both were famous for the sharpness of their wit and intellect. However, they did not merely talk about the social issues of the day – each in their own way attempted to deal with them. There is a great deal of talk these days about meeting the needs of the world's poor, but sadly much of it appears to be empty rhetoric. The poor are still very much with us and the rich are still being asked to match their rhetoric with acts of love and generosity which do not count the cost.

> *Teach us, good Lord,*
> *to serve you as you deserve,*
> *to give and not to count the cost,*
> *to fight and not to heed the wounds*
> *to toil and not to seek for rest,*
> *to labour and not to ask for any reward*
> *save that of knowing that we do your will.*
> *Amen.*
>
> Ignatius of Loyola (1491–1556)

Visions and dreams

I saw an old photograph the other day of an elderly man sitting on a wall outside a Glasgow tenement, smoking a pipe. It was one of the old tenements – graffiti on the stairs, a shirt draped over a rail – but the old man didn't see them. He was somewhere else, looking into the middle distance; he was lost in a world of his own, day-dreaming.

I wondered what this old man in the photograph was dreaming about. Was he on a flight to the past where all the love, the conversations and his 'days of sunshine' were waiting to be relived? Was he dreaming about the world as he would like it to be? Was he building castles, sailing seas, or making those 'what I *should* have said' speeches in his head? The photo reminded me of a conversation with Jimmy Reid, the Glaswegian Trades Union Leader, whose lateral thinking led to some extremely successful industrial actions; instead of strikes and 'lock-outs' he had led 'work-ins'. He had had a dream.

He spoke about the possibilities of the new technological revolution. Companies were now capable of making far greater profits than in the past, using far less labour. Therefore he dreamed of a society in which we would 'work' far fewer hours, with the profits distributed in such a way that, free from the drudgery of labour, people would be able to explore their creative potential. He dreamed of the opportunities that micro-chip technology offered to create a new Renaissance, a cultural revolution in which each contributed according to their ability and each received according to their need. Of course, that has not happened, but was he wrong to dream the dream?

Martin Luther King dreamed a dream of a day when people would not be judged by the colour of their skin but by their character, of the day when all God's children, black and white, Jews and Gentiles, Protestants and Catholics, would join hands together and sing, 'Free at last! Free at last! Thank God Almighty, we are free at last!'

Curiously, when St Peter preached about the coming of that great day he quoted a prophecy which said that, in the day of the Lord, 'Your old men shall dream dreams, and your young men shall see visions' (Joel 2.28).

Of course, people say to prophets like Jimmy Reid and Martin Luther King, 'In your dreams! Get real!' But dreams do come true. Freedom from slavery in the North American cotton plantations, independence for Gandhi's India, and the abolition of apartheid in Nelson Mandela's South Africa must have seemed like distant dreams to many people for long years, but they kept the faith, and in time, their dreams came true. So hold on to the dream and keep the faith; you never know how or when your dream might be realized.

> Lord, enable me to stand firm in the faith,
> to bear cynicism with humour and
>   fortitude.
> Save me from sanctimonious humbug.

Prevent me from pious fraud,
but let me be loyal to your gospel of love,
and let me dare to delight in its promises,
  its hope and its truth.
Amen.

Worn and flawed

Every day advertisements in magazines and on television urge us to buy potions and creams that will reduce the effects of ageing, remove wrinkles or change grey hair into a more youthful colour. If you have the money and you want to spend it on such things, you can have cosmetic surgery to remove the bags from under your eyes, at least one of your double chins, give yourself a face-lift, or lift or reshape any other bit of that is currently not 'shaping up' to your satisfaction.

For all our obsession with trying to make ourselves flawless, there is a very strong argument in favour of *im*perfections. It is our imperfections that shape our personalities, that make an individual interesting. Jesus was criticized because he spent his time with sinners, outcasts, 'imperfect' people. But those are the very people that he came to seek and save.

His disciple Peter, steeped in a tradition that believed that entry into the kingdom of God depended on following a disciplined pattern of religious observance, found it hard to come to terms with his imperfections, his failure, his denial and betrayal of Jesus. I once wrote a meditation on the Passion and resurrection of Christ in which Peter realizes why Jesus says to him, three times, 'Simon, son of John, do you love me?' In the meditation the voice of Peter says:

Suddenly I realized,
he was not rebuking me.
He was reassuring me,
that no matter how many times I failed him
he would still be recalling me into his service.
He did not expect perfection,
just my love, no matter how flawed.

Nor does Jesus expect perfection from us. He is always ready to accept our love, no matter how 'flawed' it might be.

Lord, in the generosity of your love
you embrace all my imperfections.
By your mercy, in all my relationships,
grant me the same generosity,
for your name's sake.
Amen.

You talking to me?

One of the most difficult demands on our generosity of spirit, perhaps because it weighs on the conscience, are conversations with those whose physical or mental condition make special demands on you, such as deafness, or a speech impediment. In ordinary, day-to-day relationships, it can be extremely hard to relate to someone who talks too much, who repeats the same old stories or, truth to tell, you find a bit boring.

I was once told that the most important person in your life should be the person you are talking to at any particular time. I know how put down you feel when you realize that the person you're talking to is not actually listening to you.

I can think of a head teacher who, on school open days, was so busy that he never had time to talk to anyone. When you met him, he would say 'Hello' warmly enough, but almost immediately you became aware that he was looking over your shoulder. And within seconds he would say, 'Would you excuse me, there's someone I really have to speak to, you know how it is! I'll catch up with you later.' Then with a little nod, or a pat on the arm to confirm to that he had fulfilled his duty with regard to you, he would rush off to that someone who apparently had more need of him, or was more important, or less difficult to deal with than you. Over the years I began to suspect that he said something similar to everyone he met, but it certainly didn't do a lot for one's self-esteem.

In 1987, Christy Nolan won the Whitbread Book of the Year award for his book, *Under the Eye of the Clock*. He has never been able to communicate through what we would call ordinary speech. But generous-hearted loving people in spirit listened intently to him by working hard at deciphering the code of his facial expressions, his eye movements and his body language. His book was semi-autobiographical, and through its character Joseph Christy Nolan said that it was in the faces of those who helped him to communicate, in the intensity and generosity of their patience and love for him that he 'recognized the face of God in human form'.

In a similar way, Mother Teresa of Calcutta taught her Sisters, who nurse the sick and the dying from the streets of the city, to see in the face of each person they nurse the face of the suffering Jesus.

One of the great letters of St Paul is written to the Ephesians, in which he says it was this kind of total giving, this concentration of completely unselfish love towards everyone in the life of Christ, that showed us the true nature of God. Paul said that in the light of this love we should be 'generous to one another'; we should, 'try to be like him'. Next time I meet that 'difficult' person, I shall try to remember that.

> *Lord,*
> *in the faces of all who cross my path,*
> *in the voices of those with whom I live,*
> *in the work of my colleagues,*
> *in all the people you have given me*

to know and to share my days,
may I see your face, hear your voice
and speak your words,
of healing, reconciliation, love and joy,
for your name's sake.
Amen.